Skill Building Pro

WALTER M. SHARP, PH. D.
THE OHIO STATE UNIVERSITY

·

RONALD D. JOHNSON (RETIRED)
SAM HOUSTON STATE UNIVERSITY

SOUTH-WESTERN
CENGAGE Learning

Australia • Brazil • Japan • Korea • Mexico • Singapore • Spain • United Kingdom • United States

Skill Building Pro

Walter Sharp, Ronald Johnson

VP/Editorial Director:
Jack W. Calhoun

VP/Editor-in-Chief:
Karen Schmohe

Acquisitions Editor:
Jane Phelan

Sr. Developmental Editor:
Dr. Inell Bolls

Marketing Manager:
Valerie Lauer

Marketing Coordinator:
Kelley Gilreath

Sr. Content Project Manager:
Martha Conway

Manager of Technology, Editorial:
Liz Prigge

Sr. Technology Project Manager:
Mike Jackson

Sr. Manufacturing Coordinator:
Charlene Taylor

Art Director:
Linda Helcher

Cover and Internal Designer:
Grannan Graphic Design, Ltd.

Cover Images:
Jim Calloway Photography

Photo Researcher:
John Hill

Production House:
Integra Software Services Pvt. Ltd.

Printer:
Quebecor World – Dubuque
Dubuque, IA

COPYRIGHT © 2008
South-Western, a part of Cengage
Learning.

Printed in the United States of America
3 4 5 6 7   10

ISBN 13: 978-0-538-72991-8
ISBN 10: 0-538-72991-0

ALL RIGHTS RESERVED.
No part of this work covered by the
copyright hereon may be reproduced
or used in any form or by any means—
graphic, electronic, or mechanical,
including photocopying, recording,
taping, Web distribution or information
storage and retrieval systems, or in any
other manner—without the written
permission of the publisher.

For permission to use material from this
text or product, submit a request online
at www.cengage.com/permissions

For more information about our
products, contact us at:

South-Western Cengage Learning
5191 Natorp Boulevard
Mason, Ohio 45040
USA

Contents

Part 1   Lessons 1–60

Part 2   Timed Writings 1–16

Part 3   On Your Own: Textbook Drills 1–17

Welcome to Skill Building Pro

Skill Building Pro is a new fully integrated textbook and keyboarding program designed to improve your keyboarding speed and accuracy. It includes 60 lessons of instruction as well as self-paced writings, drill practice, timed writings with error diagnostics, games for building skill, and a word processor. *Skill Building Pro* is designed for students who have learned to key by touch and who now want to increase their skill and become power typists.

The *Skill Building Pro* textbook is organized into three parts; each correlate to the software.

- **Part 1 Lessons:** Lessons designed specifically for building speed or accuracy or for assessment. Each lesson will require about 30 to 40 minutes to complete.
- **Part 2 Timed Writings:** Additional timed writings to measure your progress.
- **Part 3 On Your Own:** Individualized practice geared to your needs, including Paced Writings to build speed while maintaining accuracy, Drill Practice to improve specific reach errors you are making, Games for fun and fluency, and Technique Builders for more practice.

Getting Started with *Skill Building Pro* Software

If you are using the Student version of *Skill Building Pro*, you must first install the software on your computer. The CD is located in the back of this textbook. Refer to the Quick Start Guide for help. The first time you use the software, you will need to set up a student record. To do so, launch *Skill Building Pro*, click the New User button, and fill in the fields. If you will be using the program in a distance learning environment, select Distance Learning Course as the class and enter the **course code**, which your instructor will provide. Select this code and copy it (Ctrl + C); then paste it (Ctrl + V) into the course code field. To save your student record to a location other than the default data path, click the data path button and change the location to your flash drive or other location.

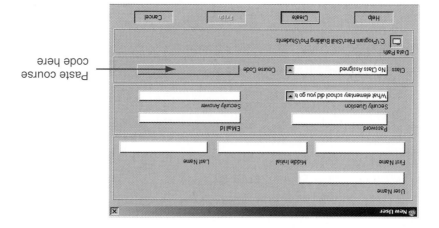

Paste course code here

When you log in to the software, you may transfer your student record from the web or another location to your current location. This allows you to update your storage device with the most recent file, whether it is stored on the web, a flash drive, or a server.

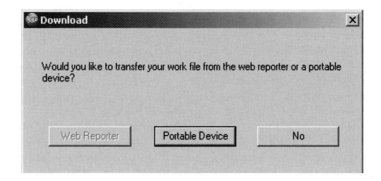

Using the Main Menu

When you have logged in, you will go to the Main menu. It includes tabs for Lessons, Timed Writings, and On Your Own; a WP button for the Word Processor; and various navigation buttons near the bottom of the screen. The tabs correlate with the three parts of the textbook.

Lessons [Lessons]

The Lesson tab provides access to 60 lessons; each cycle of ten lessons includes five lessons for building speed, four for increasing accuracy, and one for assessment. Each lesson also includes a game and ends with the Lesson Report.

SPEED LESSONS

Speed building involves challenge and quick gratification; you'll know that you are succeeding immediately. Speed building generally results in keying errors, but it's important to remember that speed is a part of good technique. The best way to increase your speed is to drive for it using excellent reach techniques; later you'll reduce your speed and concentrate on accuracy. Speed-building lessons include the following:

Warmup. The Warmup will get your attention focused on the task at hand and enable you to limber up your fingers. You will key each drill line from your textbook twice, trying to improve your speed the second time.

Technique Builder. You'll practice the common reaches in words and then key them in sentences, aiming to increase your speed by 2 words the second time.

Listen and Key. Listen to the phrase and key it as a unit; think and key words and phrases and watch your fluency improve.

Speed Sprints. Your challenge is to maintain your 15-second rate for 20 seconds. You will have only a short break between attempts, so you will need to stay focused.

1' Speed Writing. You will key for one minute to set your base rate. Then you will be challenged to push for a 4-word increase. A marker will appear on screen, showing you where you should be in the copy each quarter minute in order to meet your goal. Concentrate! You will have three chances to make your goal.

Sustained Writing. You will key two 2-minutes writings and then be challenged to maintain your average 2-minute rate for 3 minutes.

ACCURACY LESSONS

Key these lessons at a comfortable rate, slower than your highest speed. Work with a confident and focused mind-set to improve accuracy. Keying is a mental activity as much as a physical one. To succeed, relax, key at a comfortable rate, and focus on what you are keying. Accuracy lessons include these activities:

Warmup. Limber up your fingers and get focused.

Technique Builder. You will be challenged to key with one or less errors. If you do, then you'll work on fluency; if you do not, you will practice common letter pairs.

Accuracy Builder. You will have three attempts to key each sentence within the accuracy limit.

1' Accuracy Writing. After determining the 1-minute rate at which you can key within the error tolerance, you will be challenged to increase your correct words a minute (2 words are deducted from your base speed for each error). Depending on how you do, the software will challenge you to increase in either speed or accuracy.

Sustained Writing. Now you will really challenge yourself to maintain your accuracy for a longer time. You will key from the textbook for 2 minutes, and then for 3 minutes, trying to meet the goal set by your work in the software.

ASSESSMENT LESSONS

Each tenth lesson evaluates your progress. By the end of the course, you should reach a higher level with better accuracy. As you progress through the program, consider these assessment timed writings as your measure of progress to that point. Use the results to help you reach new goals. Your emphasis in an assessment lesson is control. Key at a comfortable rate and concentrate. New routines include the following:

Timed Writing. You will key two timed writings from the textbook; the default is 3'. Focus on keying accurately. These timed writing results will be a good indicator of how much you have improved in both speed and accuracy. After you finish the timed writings, you can view a diagnostic summary to see the types of errors you made.

Paced Writing. Paced Writings allow you to establish a personal base rate from which you can move your speed forward. You will work first to increase your speed and then you will drop your speed back for control. A pacing marker shows where you should be at each 15-second interval in order to meet your goals. Continue to work on paced writings outside the lesson as described below.

Timed Writings `Timed Writings`

Part 2 of your textbook contains additional timed writings. In the software, you can access these from the Timed Writings tab on the main screen. Select the Timed Writing and the length of time you want to key. You will key from the textbook. When you are done, your speed will display on screen and the errors will be marked for you to review. This information will also be added to your cumulative diagnostic summary for your review.

The results of your three best timed writings for 1', 2', 3', and 5' as well as the results of your last 20 timed writings appear in the Timed Writing Report. Click on the various timings to display your keystrokes and errors.

Errors made on timed writings are tracked by row, finger, and type. From the Menu bar, choose Reports and then Error Diagnostic Report to see the kind of errors you are making. Drill Practice provides intensive practice to improve accuracy problems.

On Your Own `On Your Own`

Skill Building Pro includes four types of practice that you can do on your own: Paced Writings, Drill Practice, Textbook Drills, and Games.

PACED WRITINGS

The Paced Writing feature, designed to build your keyboarding speed while maintaining accuracy, consists of ten paragraph sets. *Skill Building Pro* uses one set for each pacing cycle. A complete pacing cycle consists of a speed cycle and accuracy cycle, each with three levels. The paced writings help you work toward improving your base speed by 6 *gwam* (gross words a minute) for each set.

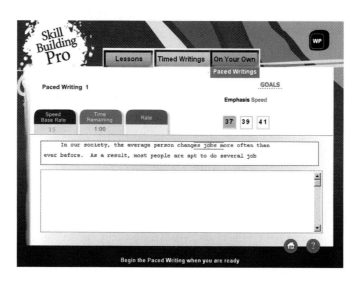

Paced Writings are keyed for one minute. The program automatically divides the number of words you are striving to key into 15-second goals. The range of characters where you should be at each quarter minute is identified between horizontal lines (pacing markers). In the speed cycle, you must increase your speed 2 *gwam* and also key at a steady pace as indicated by the pacing markers until you reach a 6 *gwam* increase. In the Accuracy Cycle, your speed goal is reduced to 2 *gwam* below the overall speed goal you just achieved. Now you must key accurately as well as meet your speed and pacing goals. This routine continues until you increase your speed 6 *gwam* and key within the accuracy limit. Then the program brings up new source copy and the process repeats at your new base rate.

Paced Writings are also available in the Assessment lessons. You progress sequentially through the Paced Writings, with your goals building based on your earlier work. *Skill Building Pro* remembers where you are in the Paced Writings, whether you access them through a lesson or from the On Your Own tab.

Try to key Paced Writings for 10 to 15 minutes during each keyboarding session to see the most improvement in your skill.

DRILL PRACTICE

Drill Practice allows you to choose drill lines in the area on which you need to focus, such as Adjacent Key, Concentration, Direct Reach, by letter or finger, and more. When you take a timed writing, your errors are recorded in a Diagnostic Report. *Skill Building Pro* keeps track of the types of errors you make, and tells you which area needs the most work. When you go into Drill Practice, one of the sections will be marked as your top priority. But you can choose to key in any tab within Drill Practice that you want.

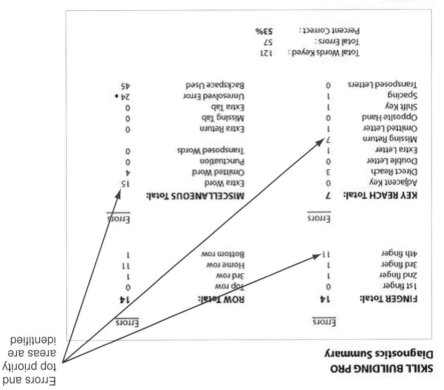

SKILL BUILDING PRO
Diagnostics Summary

Errors and top priority areas are identified

FINGER Total:	14	ROW Total:	14
Errors		*Errors*	
1st finger	0	Top row	0
2nd finger	1	3rd row	1
3rd finger	1	Home row	11
4th finger	11	Bottom row	1

KEY REACH Total:	7	MISCELLANEOUS Total:	15
Errors		*Errors*	
Adjacent Key	0	Extra Word	15
Direct Reach	3	Omitted Word	4
Double Letter	0	Punctuation	0
Extra Letter	1	Transposed Words	0
Missing Return	7	Extra Return	0
Omitted Letter	1	Missing Tab	0
Opposite Hand	0	Extra Tab	0
Shift Key	1	Unresolved Error	24 •
Spacing	1	Backspace Used	45
Transposed Letters	0		

Total Words Keyed :	121
Total Errors :	57
Percent Correct :	53%

NOTES:
• **Top priority**
Use the concentration drills to correct: extra letters, transposed letters, extra words, omitted words, punctuation, transposed words, extra returns, and missing returns.

TEXTBOOK DRILLS

The third part of your textbook contains a variety of technique drills for you to complete for extra practice. Textbook Drills focus on specific techniques. The drills are keyed from the textbook (pages 128–134). Your *gwam*, errors, and total lines keyed are reported in your Summary Report.

GAMES

Skill Building Pro has two games that are part of the lessons. You can also access them from the On Your Own tab. Both games require that you do some keying in order to play the game. In Guess It, you key drill lines to earn chances to solve the puzzle. In Jump One, you key drill lines to earn time to play the peg-jumping game.

WORD PROCESSOR

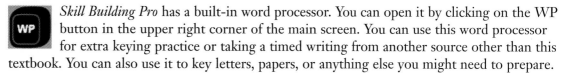

Skill Building Pro has a built-in word processor. You can open it by clicking on the WP button in the upper right corner of the main screen. You can use this word processor for extra keying practice or taking a timed writing from another source other than this textbook. You can also use it to key letters, papers, or anything else you might need to prepare.

Reports

Reports are available from the Menu bar. *Skill Building Pro* includes a number of different reports to allow you to easily track your progress. You can see how you did in individual lessons, obtain a comprehensive summary of your timed writings, view the diagnostic summary, and more. The Student Performance Report gives a detailed report of your progress and links to specific Lesson Reports and completed timed writings. The Lesson Reports are available at the end of each lesson.

SKILL BUILDING PRO
Student Performance Record   Page 1

Lesson #	Date Completed	Lesson Type	Timed/Sustained Writings		
			Length	Attempt 1	Attempt 2
1	030506 11:13am	Speed	1min	56/1	58/0
2	030506 05:07pm	Speed	1 min	83/1	85/1
3	030506 05:53pm	Speed	1 min	83/1	85/1
4	030506 06:20pm	Speed	1 min	83/1	85/1
5	030506 08:42pm	Speed	1 min	83/1	85/1
6	030506 07:40pm	Speed	1 min	83/1	85/1
7	030506 06:25pm	Speed	1 min	83/1	85/1
8	030506 03:30pm	Speed	1 min	83/1	85/1
9	030506 06:42pm	Speed	1 min	83/1	85/1
10	030506 05:25pm	Speed	1 min	83/1	85/1

Best 1' Timed Writings

#	Writing	Date	Length	Backspace Allowed	GWAM	Errors
1	How Modules	030506 11:13am	1:00	yes	52	2
2	Test3	030506 05:07pm	1:00	yes	12	1
3	Test2	030506 05:53pm	1:00	yes	5	0
4	Test1	030506 06:20pm	1:00	yes	8	3
5	Test4	030506 08:42pm	1:00	yes	5	0

Software Navigation

The other buttons that you see on the *Skill Building Pro* software screen are probably similar to buttons that you are familiar with from other software programs. The Home button will take you back to the Main menu. The Help button is always available. When you click it, it will open up the Help system and display information about the screen you are on. There are also buttons to print, to logout, and to exit the program.

Skill Building Pro at Home

Skill Building Pro also allows you to manage your files in a distance learning environment. You can work exclusively from home, and use the upload button to send your work to your instructor.

Connect to the Internet and then click the Upload button shown at the left to send your student record to the Web Reporter. Your instructor may add comments to your reports. For further details, go to www.cengage.com/keyboarding/sharp.

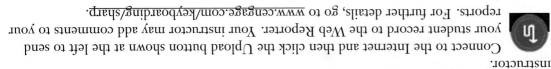

Exit

Help

Logout

Print

Part

1

Start where you are and believe where you will be at the finish!

DRILL 15
Weak Fingers

Follow the standard directions on page 128.

Outside Reaches

1 paws quiz zeal was quake say quack spa upon polite zone pay saw police
2 People are being quickly sent to aid the poor citizens in their ports.
3 Zona's zest was zapped after she got that zero on the quiz in zoology.

4 Xavier exited quickly and took a taxi to my Sixty-Sixth Street duplex.
5 Paul watched the pleasant haze go away near the troop's practice zone.
6 Did either Peter or Paul quip that reporters made the zone impassable?

DRILL 16
Rows

Follow the standard directions on page 128.

Bottom Row

1 Recent bank embezzlements now exceed the maximum government estimates.
2 Fox, mink, and/or zebra are common animals in Nevada and Montana zoos.
3 Anorexia, common in young women, is characterized by aversion to food.

4 Calvin Bonn took a maximum of six dozen zinnias and a minimum of mums.
5 Xavier was excited to vacation in Bavaria and visit vacant zinc mines.
6 Dr. Betz gave him an extensive physical examination on Monday morning.

Top Row

7 Pete said he will work at the pet store this week for his two sisters.
8 Perry, you were to type quietly the two erudite reports that were due.
9 Terry wrote a quarterly report; Pete wrote a witty query to the paper.

10 I tried to write the report on the proper ways to prepare turtle soup.
11 Either Terry or Peter tore the dirty papers off the exquisite picture.
12 We were there with two witty reporters who tried to write wordy quips.

DRILL 17
Direct Reaches

Follow the standard directions on page 128.

1 June obtained unusual services from a number of celebrated decorators.
2 No doubt my brother Cecil served as an umpire on that bright June day.
3 Bryce found a large brown bag of junk and dumped much of it on my bed.
4 Kathryn hunted in many places for recent survey projections on hunger.

5 Cecil Vunderink, my brother, broke my brush; he has too much strength.
6 Lanny recorded my check and processed my payment faster than expected.
7 Joyce is the young nurse in that funny brown and grey checked uniform.
8 Junior told my grandmother he received my gift before any other gifts.

9 My brother, Mervyn, has my army clothing; Bernice has my other things.
10 Cec and Ty browsed in many craft shops and found numerous funny items.
11 I doubt that Gretta brought many second-rate musicians to my musicale.
12 My brother wrote the hymns sung by Cecilia; he writes excellent music.

LESSON 1

Speed Emphasis

1a Warmup

Directions Key each line twice from the textbook. Strive for accuracy the first time and try to improve your speed or fluency the second time.

alphabet 1 Crazy clowns jumped over Killer, the quivering brown fox terrier.
fig/sym 2 The total due is $1094.00, the sum of $345.00, $260.00 & $489.00.
speed 3 After they left, four cadets jogged just past the old polo field.

1b TECHNIQUE BUILDER

Directions Key from the software screen. You will practice common letter pairs and then strive to increase your speed.
Goal Increase speed by 2 *gwam* and stay within the error limit.

 Key Point | Digraphs are any two-letter combinations. Each combination requires a different physical movement. Practicing common digraphs helps you key two-letter combinations quickly.

1c LISTEN AND KEY

Directions Listen to the phrase, and then key it as a single unit. Key the space following a word as part of the word.
Option Key the phrases as they flash on your screen.

10 and the | and the | and the | and the date | and the date | and the date is
11 if he | if he is | if he is paid | if he is paid | he is ready | to go home
12 bid for | may bid for | may bid for the chance | did she | did she add it

1d SPEED SPRINTS

Directions Key from the software screen. You will have a limited time between attempts before the next timing begins. Keep focused.
Goal Strive to maintain your 15" speed on three 20" timings.

Timely Topic

© COMSTOCK IMAGES

Building Keyboarding Skill

First, technique; then speed; and finally accuracy. Experts who have studied learning a skill support this order of skill development, whether the skill is soccer, golf, or keyboarding. Speed is an integral part of good technique. As you strive to build speed, apply good techniques:

- Eyes on copy to be keyed
- Fingers curved
- Wrists low but not touching the keyboard
- Forearms parallel to the keyboard
- Body erect; feet flat on the floor.

You will begin with each speed lesson with untimed practice to gain confidence and fluency. Then each lesson will guide, pace, and challenge you to key beyond your comfort level. Realize that when speed is emphasized, errors increase. When accuracy is emphasized, speed drops. If you're not making mistakes in the speed lessons, you're concentrating too much on accuracy.

DRILL 13
Opposite Hand

Follow the standard directions on page 128.

 **Key Point** | Concentration is critical to accurate keying.

t/y

1 trip thirst retest taught pretext contract greatest attitude southwest
2 you yearly enjoy boy yoga query mayonnaise mayor pyre essay myriad yes
3 Usually each type of symphony results in ostentation by young soloist.

o/w

4 onto opt took oppose proctor moreover condition professors corporation
5 weed with pewter weather sweetest brewers awesome workweek wheelbarrow
6 I know the wording of the weird weather report won't worry the coward.

g/h

7 budget luggage plague gauge glide ground guide gumption guitar grounds
8 how think thrill shall chills shallow much crunch watch thunder throng
9 Vaughn bought the lightweight luggage, bandana, and guitar from Holly.

i/e

10 ignore idea slim this milk kindly identify immerse imports ice signal
11 escape engrave entire ebony emblem enter enterprise engine melt easel
12 A dedicated editor decided to edit the edict addressed to the author.

Check your skill

13 Twenty youthful yeomen ate teriyaki and yogurt in the windy courtyard.
14 Be slow to use any new words until you know how to use them correctly.
15 Gregory thought that the myth about night terrorism might yet be true.
16 Eight editors believed special diets were effective for losing weight.

DRILL 14
Concentration: Long Words

Follow the standard directions on page 128.

1 development possibility agreement circumstance maximum successful
2 approximately administrations political innovations relationships

3 geographical universal epidermis exasperates mutilating genealogy
4 acupuncture astound verbiage graffito vernacular optic exemptions

5 environmental prohibitive volatile poisonous malevolent unpopular
6 enunciation archaeologist opportunities quixotic analyzed conquer

7 vitamins handicap solvent vernacular mediate cleverly susceptible
8 linguist intimate satirical billboards petroleum artificial waxes

9 By February the gubernatorial candidate mustered minimal support.
10 Gratification is achieved by one's deep commitment to excellence.

Directions

1. Take a 1' timing; key from the textbook. If you finish before time is up, begin again.
2. Repeat the timing 3 more times, trying to increase your rate. Key from the screen.
   A marker will indicate where you need to be at the end of each 15" in order to reach your goal.
   You will have 10" between attempts.

gwam 1'

	gwam
A trip to the mountains is a great experience. The solitude	12
can be very healing to one who must spend a great deal of time in	25
the public eye or work long hours in an office. Here, there is a	39
chance for one to get pleasure from just lazy walks along one of	52
the many trails, to hear the different sounds all around you, to	65
fish at a quiet stream, or to reach the top and gaze at the beauti-	78
ful view. If you plan well, the mountains can offer you a special	91
world and something you will want to remember for the rest of your	105
life. Perhaps you should begin planning your trip now.	116

1' | 1 | 2 | 3 | 4 | 5 | 6 | 7 | 8 | 9 | 10 | 11 | 12 | 13 |

1f SUSTAINED WRITING

E

Directions

1. Key a 2' writing, beginning with paragraph 1. Key from the textbook.
2. Key another 2' writing, beginning with paragraph 2. If you finish before time is up, start over with paragraph 1. Key from the textbook.
3. Key a 3' writing on the entire writing. Try to maintain your average 2' rate.

gwam 3'

	gwam
We like our life as we do because we were programmed that	4
way. Our society evolves all the time with clear changes going on	8
every four to five years. For example, as we quickly whiz through	13
our teen years, music is often an item just ready to be set. When	17
it occurs, it sets the kind of music we like to hear for the rest	22
of our lives. Many forces can affect our choice when it is our	26
time to be programmed for music. We can be affected by the factors	30
of our situation, including our family, our closest friends, and	35
the music in style at the time.	37
The choice of the kind of music we like to hear is exciting	41
because there are so many types of quality music. To name a few,	45
we may choose from modern, jazz, rap, folk, country, rock, or a	50
blend of each. Within each type, there is always new music to	54
like. Rock music had its start in the middle of the last century;	58
it passed through about a ten-stage period beginning with rock and	63
roll and coming to an end with pop rock. Ask people what kind of	67
music they like. You can then work out just about how old they	71
must be. Remember that they have been programmed.	75

3' | 1 | 2 | 3 | 4 |

DRILL 11

Specific Row

Follow the standard directions on page 128.

Third Row: Keep wrists low.

1 quote report were port riot error trip tree quit wire worry write poor
2 may cut buy ten fix bike new tire quit my be quiet no review rezone it
3 Word processing applications require much patience and skill to learn.
4 We quit to write our tour trip report while you were at the port riot.

Home Row: Keep fingers curved and upright.

5 all day dad ask a laugh glass jar had half shall fade safe as has said
6 hall lash gas dad has staff half fad glad shall flag glass flash false
7 Dallas sold jade flasks and dishes; Al has a glass flask full of sage.
8 Sally Ash has a faded glass doll. Josh Jakes was a sad lad last fall.

Bottom Row

9 many woman men relax back my van a lazy man move my cable my zinc mine
10 no vacancy named number many zone can back extra taxes become a banker
11 No exact number of zoning changes can be made by civic voting members.
12 A man and a woman came to exchange a dozen boxes of venison on Monday.

DRILL 12

Opposite Hand

Follow the standard directions on page 128.

Identical reaches with the opposite hands often cause errors. Concentrate to key accurately.

k/d

1 keep keen keg kayak kale keno keepsake kerchief kennel kernel kerosene
2 drag mind ride made dive ahead drove trade proud riddle riding discuss
3 Dozens of ducks dunked up or down in a murky pool near the drawbridge.

e/i

4 each erupt verse excess equal evade texture yearn ever exponent server
5 idol inch ionic incurs impair imprint lining inlaid imply input twists
6 Neither niece received notice of their vacancies in the science field.

s/l

7 is so was say same sale basic ideas salary to test east vast tell slot
8 also sale slip slot self tells shall slowly slump lease please enclose
9 Allison fell asleep on a small slope of a hillside close to the falls.

r/u

10 ran rob door drive prove are dart rent freight hard jar car sort train
11 tube ugly would quest annual astute unusual unified counties education
12 Rheumatoid arthritis, bursitis, and neuritis caused the ulcer to hurt.

Check your skill

13 The lackadaisical student was asked to dust the book on the bookstand.
14 Neither niece received notice of their vacancies in the science field.
15 The atlas also listed telescopes and kaleidoscopes as essential tools.
16 Our resolutions requested usury rules be resurrected for underwriters.

LESSON 2   Speed Emphasis

2a Warmup

Directions Key each line twice from the textbook. Strive for accuracy the first time and try to improve your speed or fluency the second time.

alphabet 1 Bold quotes picked from a few excellent acts amazed Judge Harvey.

fig/sym 2 My scores of 65%, 73%, 82%, 94%, and 100% averaged 82.8%—or a B.

speed 3 She tricked him into picking the long icicle along the icy trail.

2b TECHNIQUE BUILDER

Directions Key from the software screen. You will practice common letter pairs and then strive to increase your speed.
Goal Increase speed by 2 *gwam* and stay within the error limit.

or en ti 4 oranges accord anchor endure fence fifteen time renting twentieth

or en ti 5 When you know the end of the story, it is time for a new subject.

es nd te 6 esteem addresses ashes pound command fondly after acute templates

es nd te 7 If everyone in a committee agrees, you may have the wrong agenda.

to nt is 8 today button auto agents account cents crisis islands risk tennis

to nt is 9 To contribute to a worthy cause is one way to make a happy heart.

2c LISTEN AND KEY

Directions Listen to the phrase, and then key it as a single unit. Key the space following a word as part of the word.
Option Key the phrases as they flash on your screen.

10 as we | as we try | as we try we see | we see that we are | able to begin

11 as soon | as soon as | as soon as we | as soon as we go | to my own house

12 the dial | the dial is | the dial is worn out | the dial is worn out by

2d SPEED SPRINTS

Directions Key from the software screen. You will have a limited time between attempts before the next timing begins. Keep focused.
Goal Strive to maintain your 15" speed on three 20" timings.

 Key Point | The fastest and easiest words to type are balanced-hand words. Every other letter in the word is struck by a finger on the opposite hand.

13 They may wish to have the six men pay and work for the ornaments.

balanced hand 14 Maury asked Jane if she got cocoa for the neighbor or the worker.

15 Pay the eight men for all the work; they may go to town to visit.

DRILL 9
Special Reaches

Follow the standard directions on page 128.

Goal
Improve special reaches.

Key Point | Work for smooth stroking. Avoid pauses but do not reach for speed.

Direct Reaches: Reaches with the same finger; keep hands quiet.

1 Barb saw many hybrids at the fairgrounds–hydrangea, hyacinth, grapes.
2 Unless I get multiple discounts, any price for brass is not a bargain.
3 Volumes of excellent municipal records were a target of annual thefts.
4 That brilliant young graduate counted a hundred brochures on eclipses.

Adjacent Keys: Keep fingers curved and upright.

5 Three guides loped in a column as we stalked over trails after a lion.
6 We condemn her notion that we can buy excellent behavior with rewards.
7 As Louise Liu said, few questioned the points asserted by the porters.
8 People acquire few rewards from walking short treks to Union Terminal.

Double Letters: Tap keys rapidly.

9 Anna will see that Jill accepts an assignment in the office next week.
10 Joann and Buzz will carry those bookkeeping supplies to Judd's office.
11 Lynn's committee supplied food and coffee for the Mississippi meeting.
12 The school committee will do well to pass on all the Tennessee offers.

DRILL 10
Specific Fingers

Follow the standard directions on page 128.

Key Point | Reinforce correct key locations and reaches; keep hands quiet as you make long reaches.

First Finger

1 fun jam run try van from gray home hung hymn that very bone brings gym
2 my by just turn fib try hard grab hat many hard bargain very foggy eve
3 Rhett gets just one great big bag of free things from them every week.
4 Helen thought Teri's story about the very bad storm might not be true.

Third Finger

5 up put top pop two your yoyo were tire quite quote quiet teeter terror
6 so soon was slow low solo looks well was lost six pales polls all zaps
7 L. W. Low saw six extra people mop, wax, and polish all of the floors.
8 All old notices I saw are too low on our list to allow for good sales.

Fourth Finger

9 takers of the prizes to doze lazily in a daze a hazy day pass the quiz
10 pass quite zeal zap acquire past quell cozy top quaint zealot as quirk
11 They were quite polite to the witty reporter who requested your story.
12 Pam is too zapped to puzzle whether to postpone a paper or pass it on.

2e 1' SPEED WRITING ↑ ↑

E

Directions

1. Take a 1' timing; key from the textbook. If you finish before time is up, begin again.
2. Repeat the timing 3 more times, trying to increase your rate. Key from the screen.
   A marker will indicate where you need to be at the end of each 15" in order to reach your goal.
   You will have 10" between attempts.

gwam 1'

As you key this copy, try to keep your eyes from moving from	12
the copy to the screen or to your hands. It is common to use speed	26
and accuracy as a means to measure your skill. Both speed and	38
accuracy require you to keep your eyes fixed on the copy. In the	51
learning process, however, emphasis is made on just one or the	64
other, not both at the same time. The two come together when you	77
reach your goal for the speed you wish to key. Looking away from	90
your copy can only cause you to lose your place or time.	101

1' | 1 | 2 | 3 | 4 | 5 | 6 | 7 | 8 | 9 | 10 | 11 | 12 | 13 |

2f SUSTAINED WRITING

E

Directions

1. Key a 2' writing, beginning with paragraph 1. Key from the textbook.
2. Key another 2' writing, beginning with paragraph 2. If you finish before time is up, start
   over with paragraph 1. Key from the textbook.
3. Key a 3' writing on the entire writing. Try to maintain your average 2' rate.

gwam 3'

In a democracy, you have the right to vote on the issues and	4
the people who run your government. This places the job of being	8
informed upon the people. So, just as soon as you can, 'you are	13
expected to register to vote. Yet, having the right to vote is one	17
thing; to make a learned choice with each vote is another. Before	22
going to the polls, study all the issues and try to know the quali-	26
ties of each person whose names will appear on the ballot. Only	30
then can you say you have done a good job as a citizen.	34
Most of us realize that some of the best ways to learn more	38
about each person and any issue to be voted upon are to listen to	43
the radio and TV and to read the newspaper. Be aware that there	47
may be some bias in the media. In some towns and cities, there are	51
public meetings where you can see and ask questions of a candidate.	56
Quite often, you are exposed to more facts than you care to hear or	60
read about. Just be sure you are ready to vote in a way that truly	65
is what you think is best for you and your country.	69

3' | 1 | 2 | 3 | 4 |

DRILL 6
Long Reaches

Follow the standard directions on page 128.

Key Point Reach with the fingers; keep hands still.

1 sold code much many loan vice side cent thus told fund wide price
2 slow gift grow golf cloth delay demand broke checks chance manual
3 Bradley broke his left thumb after lunch on a great hunting trip.

4 brand much cent cease numb bright brief music jump special carved
5 music brown hence forums enemy bright fold signed editor specific
6 Vera and I brag about her great music talent, but June is humble.

7 lunch great jump my hunt record young brave many curved cent pump
8 nerve mumps create zany mystic curve annual any check brag brunch
9 Junior received maximum respect by being humble, not by bragging.

DRILL 7
Adjacent Fingers

Follow the standard directions on page 128.

1 yule western quit action poker ask polka were quiet tree pony sad
2 dues which plans claim giving during five vote else thanks always
3 Guy Klien is a great polo player, but steroids ruined his health.

4 into mail plan give this time might find help sent item high file
5 civil quiet inform plant blank furnish quality single wishes quit
6 Trent and Lois said they were going to try to take polka lessons.

DRILL 8
One-Handed Words

Follow the standard directions on page 128.

1 kill pin my ploy milk junk monk limp joy jump kimono mill holy in
2 web garage wax zest zebra treat serve brew test debate decree red
3 ace ill are lip bar mom dad nil ear oil fad pop cab upon were hip

4 mill ply moon hulk imply ink poll link loop lymph mink yolk polio
5 rest were draw crave great extra craze excel draft weeds rage red
6 rag hip beg sat hop sew ink tag joy tea mop wax pin web noun seat

7 I gave him my opinion on a great estate tax case we read at noon.
8 Rebecca gave Phillip a great award after we gave him a brass bed.
9 Teresa saw Barbara start a debate on a minimum tax on a monopoly.

10 Wendy and Kris paid dearly to ship the overweight box I received.
11 Kaye and Freddy received an activity guide prior to leaving home.
12 That mangy dog grabbed the fish and jumped into the lake with it.

Speed Emphasis

3a Warmup

Directions Key each line twice from the textbook. Strive for accuracy the first time and try to improve your speed or fluency the second time.

alphabet 1 Tex was quite amazed over just how big key crops are off my land.

fig/sym 2 Out-of-state checks #14 ($38) and #16 ($790) were honored on 2/5.

speed 3 Please assist me at my site so we can rotate and patrol the area.

3b TECHNIQUE BUILDER

Directions Key from the software screen. You will practice common letter pairs and then strive to increase your speed.
Goal Increase speed by 2 *gwam* and stay within the error limit.

ed ur of 4 debated bedrooms ended urged burns blur officers profits softball

ed ur of 5 I urge the editor of the tour guide to edit the proof copy again.

it ar ha 6 item auditor admitted are barn cellar area happiest chances alpha

it ar ha 7 It is easy for an artist to have a chat if the subject is on art.

st ng se 8 stands frosty almost needing changes dining seconds himself arise

st ng se 9 Adjusting to seeing oneself staying calm in a storm is very hard.

3c LISTEN AND KEY

Directions Listen to the phrase, and then key it as a single unit. Key the space following a word as part of the word.
Option Key the phrases as they flash on your screen.

 Key Point | Dictation is an external way of pacing your keying speed. The objective is to key phrases, not letter by letter or word by word. Think phrases and watch your speed grow.

10 as soon | as soon as | as soon as the | if it | if it did | if it did agree

11 if it rains | if it rains I | if it rains I am | if it rains I am going

12 of them | the world | to handle | to handle problems | to handle problems

3d SPEED SPRINTS

Directions Key from the software screen. You will have a limited time between attempts before the next timing begins. Keep focused.
Goal Strive to maintain your 15" speed on three 20" timings.

13 He may sign the forms by proxy if they make an audit of the firm.

balanced hand 14 It is their wish to pay them for land maps of eight island towns.

15 Did they make the right title forms for the eight big name firms?

DRILL 4
Spelling Demons

Follow the standard directions on page 128.

1 accommodates accidentally acknowledge adequacy aghast accelerates
2 all right altogether apologize allotment argument auxiliary a lot
3 benefited brilliant beneficiary biennial buoyancy bankruptcy bide

4 calendar concede commitment committed consensus changeable crisis
5 develop development dignitary decision desperate debatable diesel
6 envelopes equipped erroneous existence enough energize exorbitant

7 February familiar fascinate forcible foresee forty freight fierce
8 gauge government guaranteed ghastly gaily gnawing guarantee gauze
9 happens health hygiene hindrance harass hors d'oeuvres hemorrhage

10 issue irrelevant irresistible idiosyncrasy inoculate incidentally
11 jealous judgment jurors jujitsu juxtaposition jeopardize judicial
12 keen knowledge knives batik karate ukuleles likelihood bankruptcy

13 laughable license listening lonely liaison larynx likable livable
14 management mediocrity movable mortgage maneuver magician monopoly
15 necessary noticing noticeable nickel nobody nucleus ninety nuance

DRILL 5
Spelling Demons

Follow the standard directions on page 128.

1 obstacle organize original opulent occurrence occasional occurred
2 persuade precede privilege preceding pageants phenomenal publicly
3 questionnaire quantity quality quotient query plaque opaque queue
4 recipient remembers redundancy rhythm righteous receipt resistant
5 seize success souvenirs separate similar salable strategy sizable

6 truly temporary traceable thousandths temperaments trite thorough
7 uniform unanimous unparallel umbrella unfortunately usable budget
8 vacuum vigil vegetable volume vigilance virile visible voluminous
9 withhold willful wield wholly weird weight wherever Wednesday ewe
10 exonerate exaggerate suffix prefix relaxful texture extension tic

11 yacht wives wharfs wreckage wheelchair knowledgeable idiosyncrasy
12 zucchini zenith zinnia bizarre hazard jeopardize rendezvous zeros
13 collateral forcible adviser connoisseur plagiarism absence climbs
14 analyze contagious committee surprise unconscious embarrass issue
15 compatible definitely participation cavalry personnel sovereignty

3e 1' SPEED WRITING ↑ ↑

Directions

1. Take a 1' timing; key from the textbook. If you finish before time is up, begin again.
2. Repeat the timing 3 more times, trying to increase your rate. Key from the screen. A marker will indicate where you need to be at the end of each 15" in order to reach your goal. You will have 10" between attempts.

E

	gwam	1'

Jane and Dorothy were very good friends. In all the years — 12
they had known each other, they had a falling out only two times. — 25
The first time was when they were very young, and the subject was — 38
Jim and his new car. There was a goof on his part. The girls — 51
agreed to go riding at the same time, and there was anger for quite — 64
some time when the error came to light. The next time came many — 77
years later. Their children were the cause of an issue. The kids — 91
were angry over the rules of a game that they were playing. Even — 104
with these two problems, Jane and Dorothy were very good friends — 117
for many more years. They continue to be good friends today. — 129

1' | 1 | 2 | 3 | 4 | 5 | 6 | 7 | 8 | 9 | 10 | 11 | 12 | 13 |

3f SUSTAINED WRITING

Directions

1. Key a 2' writing, beginning with paragraph 1. Key from the textbook.
2. Key another 2' writing, beginning with paragraph 2. If you finish before time is up, start over with paragraph 1. Key from the textbook.
3. Key a 3' writing on the entire writing. Try to maintain your average 2' rate.

E

	gwam	3'

Many teachers now see the need to return to what some call an — 4
education based on quality of life. Teachers need to stress more — 9
than just the content of each text for a course. Students must — 13
know other facts to help them think with logic. They need to learn — 17
more than one point of view to help them make up their own minds. — 22
They must learn how to get along with and respect the rights of — 26
others in this world. They need to learn to not be selfish by — 30
always taking from others; but that their zenith in life should — 35
include giving to others. — 36

As a student, you must learn to have respect for yourself be- — 40
fore you can have respect for others. Do you always try to set a — 45
good example for others by doing the right thing? Do others trust — 49
you? Do they honor your word? Do you always keep your promise to — 54
do something? Do you help others without being asked? Do you try — 58
to keep both a healthy mind and body? Do you have a zest for liv- — 62
ing that shows in all that you do? How you answer these questions — 67
may reveal just how well you are able to get along with other peo- — 71
ple in the world. — 72

3' | 1 | 2 | 3 | 4 |

On Your Own

→ → →

DRILL 1
Letters a-h

Directions for Textbook Drills
1. Select the **On Your Own** tab and scroll to select **Textbook Drills**.
2. From the **Select Exercise** window, choose the exercise to practice.
3. Key each line once, working for accuracy. Try to key each line without a mistake. Repeat the drill, beginning with the first line, if desired.
4. Click **Done** to end the exercise; GWAM and errors are reported.
5. Save the exercise if desired. Results will be displayed in the Student Performance Report.

Concentrate on correct key locations. Focus on keying with fluency and control.

a 1 As an auditor, Ann asked to audit all the auto agency's antiques.

b 2 Bill Burke bid for both the blue bicycle and a bent, brass bugle.

c 3 Chances are that chap will succeed their current committee chair.

d 4 Did Dave dial the Darnels yet to discuss my dismal downtown dorm?

e 5 Eight elders may enrich the endowment to enlarge the entitlement.

f 6 The focus of the flap is over the fox and your fowl in the field.

g 7 The giggling girls gladly gathered with their guru in their glen.

h 8 Henry Hale hopes to hang his handiwork with a hearth in his home.

DRILL 2
Letters i-p

Follow the standard directions shown above.

i 9 The idealistic islander was irked over the issue of independence.

j 10 Jake enjoyed his junky jeep during his junior year at Jackson CC.

k 11 Ken Kalthoff kept several keys to a kennel locked in the kitchen.

l 12 That lame lamb loved the lair and made little effort to leave it.

m 13 Merry Maire may manage to move Moriah, a marine mammal, to Miami.

n 14 Neither Nathan nor Nelson knew the new announcer on that network.

o 15 Opal opted to open a coop to pool school books for the orphanage.

p 16 The pair pawned the paisley print pots and pocketed their profit.

DRILL 3
Letters q-z

Follow the standard directions shown above.

q 17 He quickly acquired a quantity of quarters for the quiet quartet.

r 18 Raul reasoned that a rigorous routine was right for Randi Rogers.

s 19 She suddenly saw the slant of the sleigh as it slid off sideways.

t 20 They thought through your theory and threw out anything unworthy.

u 21 Undoubtedly Ursula will understand the urgency of your situation.

v 22 The visitor viewed the visual aid and vowed to improve it vastly.

w 23 We wanted our workbox so we could work on the wobbly wheelchairs.

x 24 Xavier did pay extra to exhibit an extensive array of xylophones.

y 25 Yesterday many youths said they have yet to learn to yodel daily.

z 26 Zachary dizzily zigzagged through the maze and won a fuzzy prize.

LESSON 4

Speed Emphasis

4a Warmup

Directions Key each line twice from the textbook. Strive for accuracy the first time and try to improve your speed or fluency the second time.

alphabet	1	Virj's award is a prize as their quickest, most flexible gymnast.
fig/sym	2	Yi's Bookstore (293-555-0187) has 40% off on all paperback books.
speed	3	Just give us a candid answer as to the status of that other item.

4b TECHNIQUE BUILDER

Directions Key from the software screen. You will practice common letter pairs and then strive to increase your speed.
Goal Increase speed by 2 *gwam* and stay within the error limit.

 Key Point | Your challenge is to attain speed on digraphs, the smallest keying elements possible. This is both a mental and physical challenge.

| yo ve co | 4 | yourselves surveyors embryo cave event diver coach scopes tobacco |
| yo ve co | 5 | Beyond this canyon you'll be overcome by the beauty you discover. |

| al le me | 6 | alert health ideal ledgers blend legible amend daytime measurable |
| al le me | 7 | Having a goal to learn all I possibly can should make me erudite. |

| as io ce | 8 | asking classes seas ion captions audio certainly chances spaceman |
| as io ce | 9 | Ideas with good intentions can succeed if diligence is also used. |

4c LISTEN AND KEY

Directions Listen to the phrase, and then key it as a single unit. Key the space following a word as part of the word.
Option Key the phrases as they flash on your screen.

	10	look for	look for happy	look for happy times	look for happy times
	11	if they	if they go	if they go with them	did she	did she plan well
	12	he or she	but it is	pay for it	to the west	to the left	to the end

4d SPEED SPRINTS

Directions Key from the software screen. You will have a limited time between attempts before the next timing begins. Keep focused.
Goal Strive to maintain your 15" speed on three 20" timings.

	13	The key social work may end if they turn down the usual aid then.
balanced hand	14	Sign the work bid forms for the six men to do the city dock work.
	15	The eight auto firms own the big sign by the downtown civic hall.

Part
3

Success and magic both happen after a lot of work.

ON YOUR OWN
TEXTBOOK DRILLS

4e 1' SPEED WRITING

E

Directions
1. Take a 1' timing; key from the textbook. If you finish before time is up, begin again.
2. Repeat the timing 3 more times, trying to increase your rate. Key from the screen. A marker will indicate where you need to be at the end of each 15" in order to reach your goal. You will have 10" between attempts.

gwam   1'

A way to stay young mentally is to keep up with all the	11
changes around you. This is true in the office when a new computer	25
or new software is added to your work. Don't fight it; be among	38
the first to use it. This is true outside the office as well.	51
Read all you can to keep up with the changes going on in the world.	65
When a new idea is heard, give it a chance to be understood. You	78
will feel young and better about yourself if you adjust to a	90
changing world.	93

1' | 1 | 2 | 3 | 4 | 5 | 6 | 7 | 8 | 9 | 10 | 11 | 12 | 13 |

4f SUSTAINED WRITING

E

Directions
1. Key a 2' writing, beginning with paragraph 1. Key from the textbook.
2. Key another 2' writing, beginning with paragraph 2. If you finish before time is up, start over with paragraph 1. Key from the textbook.
3. Key a 3' writing on the entire writing. Try to maintain your average 2' rate.

gwam   3'

Perhaps you know one or more persons who have obtained prize	4
jobs with very little effort by just being in the right place at	8
the right time. Most of us may need to write a letter to the firm	13
with whom we wish to be employed just to get our foot in the door	17
for an interview. Before you write the letter, learn all you can	22
about the company. In your letter you want to sound as if you know	26
quite a bit about their business. Often this letter is best writ-	31
ten after you have prepared a data sheet.	33
In order to write a well-prepared data sheet, the first step	37
is to zero in on every quality that will qualify you for the exact	41
job you want. Do not claim to know more than you know; yet explain	46
well what you know. Then you should group those traits by order of	50
importance using a proper form that is both unique and neat. Be	55
sure that you keep your data sheet to no more than two pages (one	59
is best), but remember to make good use of white space. Be sure	63
that your data sheet is free of any errors.	66

3' | 1 | 2 | 3 | 4 |

gwam | 3' | 5'

Small business has grown in the past decade because competition has forced our nation to rely on small business as the primary source of new jobs. The risk, however, in starting any new business may be quite high for the new business owner who makes a substantial investment of money and security in the hope of making a profit. Statistics show that large numbers of businesses fail within the first year, and more than half of all new firms will not be in operation ten years later. Entrepreneurs who survive these high odds definitely should be applauded.

	3'	5'
	4	2	69
	8	5	72
	13	8	75
	17	10	77
	21	13	80
	26	15	82
	30	18	85
	35	21	88
	37	22	89

Today the biggest risk facing a small business is how to get an unknown firm to compete in a market of large, well-established companies. For the young entrepreneur, a myriad of problems may come with starting a new business. First, he or she needs to have a keen perspective of the mechanics of opening up and operating a new business. Also, it will be very useful to have managerial expertise, an ability to sell or market products or services, and an understanding of how contingencies can be used to combat all the obstacles that face a new business owner.

	3'	5'
	41	25	92
	46	28	94
	50	30	97
	55	33	100
	59	35	102
	63	38	105
	68	41	108
	72	43	110
	75	45	112

Some people start their own businesses after finding their career objectives blocked in the firms where they work. However, before making such a decision and leaving a job, a prospective business owner has to realize that working extended hours and dealing with problems of every magnitude and type are almost always the norm. Also, to be a successful entrepreneur, a person must have good business ethics as well as know some techniques for coping with stress. To own a firm may at first look to be attractive, but it is not free of irritants.

	3'	5'
	79	47	114
	83	50	117
	88	53	120
	92	55	122
	96	58	125
	101	60	127
	105	63	130
	110	66	133
	111	67	134

3' | 1 | 2 | 3 | 4
5' | 1 | 2 | 3

LESSON 5

Speed Emphasis

5a Warmup

Directions Key each line twice from the textbook. Strive for accuracy the first time and try to improve your speed or fluency the second time.

alphabet 1 On the job Will quickly proved his zeal to excel in tree farming.
fig/sym 2 Tunt-Ho's mailed passport (#358629017) was declared lost on 4/28.
speed 3 They said the new posh resort owner remained firm over the issue.

5b TECHNIQUE BUILDER

Directions Key from the software screen. You will practice common letter pairs and then strive to increase your speed.
Goal Increase speed by 2 *gwam* and stay within the error limit.

ll de fo 4 allow call really doll deals added blade cede food comforts defog
ll de fo 5 Will a new bill be made out for the fourth desk and its delivery?

hi be ea 6 thin child hi him behind fibers globe bed early bearing plea each
hi be ea 7 To achieve, you must be eager to learn everything on the subject.

ic il ro 8 ice dictate atomic ill bill boil child roasts brown frosting root
ic il ro 9 The heroic romantic story will be available for the critics soon.

5c LISTEN AND KEY

Directions Listen to the phrase, and then key it as a single unit. Key the space following a word as part of the word.
Option Key the phrases as they flash on your screen.

10 we were in | we were in awe | we were in awe of | we were in awe of her
11 hearing is easy | listening is difficult | think about the message to
12 to listen means | one must intend to hear | or understand the message

5d SPEED SPRINTS

Directions Key from the software screen. You will have a limited time between attempts before the next timing begins. Keep focused.
Goal Strive to maintain your 15" speed on three 20" timings.

Key Point | Balanced-hand words help you to develop the muscle strength you need for maximum speed.

13 If they do make such a visit, it may end the fight for the title.
balanced hand 14 Is it their duty to fight for an amendment and risk their profit?
15 Zorn is to go for the auto keys, then go to the big lake to fish.

15

gwam 3'| 5'

Very few people would ever admit to having one or two irrational beliefs or superstitions. One person may feel concern about a black cat crossing his or her path. Another person may have to check the horoscope in the paper each day, while yet another person will avidly want to check with an astrologer. Superstitions are not based on logic but more on one's personal emotion or cultural conditioning. Although it is easy to dismiss them as absurd, only those who can break a mirror without a second thought are fully entitled to do so.

4	2	69
8	5	71
13	8	74
17	10	77
22	13	79
26	16	82
30	18	85
35	21	87
36	22	88

Historically, many superstitions have come from the time of early religions when people worshipped the elements. For example, the importance once given to fire and iron has continued today when people carry a piece of coal or a small horseshoe as a good-luck piece. In earlier times, people used to keep their fireplaces going all evening to keep the fairies warm. When moving to a new home, they would often take embers from the old fireplace to burn in their new dwelling. Housewarming parties, which occur today, are a result of this old custom.

40	24	90
44	27	93
49	29	96
53	32	98
58	35	101
62	37	104
66	40	106
71	42	109
73	44	110

A number of these beliefs are based on positive ideas rather than on simply avoiding bad conditions. Thus, many people believe good luck will follow those who find several four-leaf clovers or who carry a rabbit's foot. If a person's right ear tingles, perhaps something good is being said about that person. Nothing proves that hanging a horseshoe on a building will bring better times, that eating crusts will result in curly hair, or that rolling an egg across a field will bring a better fall harvest. However, no one said there is any reason to superstitions.

77	46	113
81	49	115
86	51	118
90	54	120
94	57	123
98	59	126
103	62	128
107	64	131
111	66	133

3' |____1____|____2____|____3____|____4____|
5' |_____1_____|_____2_____|_____3_____|

5e 1' SPEED WRITING

Directions

1. Take a 1' timing; key from the textbook. If you finish before time is up, begin again.
2. Repeat the timing 3 more times, trying to increase your rate. Key from the screen.
   A marker will indicate where you need to be at the end of each 15" in order to reach your goal. You will have 10" between attempts.

gwam 1'

Trying to have a knowing mind when looking at art can be a	12
challenge. Modern art seems to give the greatest trial. I will	25
admit there are times when I act as if I know what the picture is	38
trying to say. Sometimes I make a wrong guess, speak up, and look	52
stupid. If you have the same problem, do not say what you think so	65
quickly. Just keep nodding your head while looking at the piece of	79
art. Then when you are sure the others looking at the art also	92
don't know its meaning, say what you really think. Otherwise sim-	105
ply continue with nodding your head.	112

1' | 1 | 2 | 3 | 4 | 5 | 6 | 7 | 8 | 9 | 10 | 11 | 12 | 13 |

5f SUSTAINED WRITING

Directions

1. Key a 2' writing, beginning with paragraph 1. Key from the textbook.
2. Key another 2' writing, beginning with paragraph 2. If you finish before time is up, start over with paragraph 1. Key from the textbook.
3. Key a 3' writing on the entire writing. Try to maintain your average 2' rate.

gwam 3'

People who receive data sheets often point out that most of	4
them look and sound too much like those found in a book. You	8
should organize yours after looking at several examples. Find one	13
that seems to display your skills best. Use this example only as a	17
starting point. The best data sheet is one that uses unique ideas	22
from more than one example and builds to make your own style known.	26
Your data sheet will have the most effect if it is neat, clean,	31
easy to read, and to the point in one or two pages.	34
It is an excellent plan to use the shotgun method and mail	38
copies of your data sheet to several companies. Mail copies to the	42
ones you really prize and want to work for and for which you are	47
trained. Treat each copy as if it was an original. Use high qual-	51
ity paper with no errors in the copy, and try to make each copy	55
unique to that company. Send your picture with the data sheet.	60
Let a few days go by and then call each of the people to whom you	64
mailed a data sheet. Then ask for an appointment.	68

3' | 1 | 2 | 3 | 4 |

14

In the process of developing a business, it is extremely important to plan and organize your activities. Good planning will bring about success. In our daily lives, planning helps us to organize our actions and helps us to achieve our goals. Planning is one of the functions of management. Many owners have skills in one, if not in all, of the functional areas. It is hard to develop the skills needed to satisfy each and every area. It is a known fact that without good planning, business firms will fail. Owners realize that they do not know everything. They must depend on their personnel, plan their actions, and organize their resources. If all of this is done, then a business has a chance to succeed. It is definitely true that only the well-managed firm, one that has carefully planned its activities, will succeed in the marketplace today.

As a business becomes more complex, its activities have to be more carefully planned. How is planning defined? It is the process of determining what should be attempted to achieve the objectives of the firm. Planning is a very relevant objective of management. Planning takes place to achieve the company's goals. It involves budgeting and requires much time. It is hard for a small business owner to spend a great amount of time in the planning process. The small business owner often spends much time in solving and handing the problems that are confronting him or her on a daily basis. A small business owner can't afford to take or spend so much time in planning or organizing the activities of the business. Yet a business owner must plan in order to ensure the success of the firm.

	3'	5'
	4	2	69
	8	5	71
	13	8	74
	17	10	76
	21	13	79
	26	16	82
	30	18	84
	35	21	87
	39	23	89
	43	26	92
	48	29	95
	52	31	98
	57	34	100
	57	34	100
	61	37	103
	66	39	106
	70	42	108
	74	45	111
	79	47	113
	83	50	116
	87	52	119
	92	55	121
	96	58	124
	101	60	126
	105	63	129
	109	65	132
	110	66	132

3' | 1 | 2 | 3 | 4 |
5' | 1 | 2 | 3 |

LESSON 6

Accuracy Emphasis

6a Warmup

Directions Key each line twice from the textbook. Strive for accuracy the first time and try to improve your speed or fluency the second time.

alphabet 1 Xiomara's quickly stolen bases just helped Valez win a fine game.
fig/sym 2 Account #263-419 earned interest this year of $1,357.50 (7 7/8%).
accuracy 3 Your trustee will soon supply us with three missing installments.

6b TECHNIQUE BUILDER

Directions Key from the software screen. Additional practice lines will display if you do not meet your accuracy goal. Key accurately.

ne we wi 4 Maybe we can replace your old window with a new window next week.
ne we wi 5 neat honey gone knee weeks flowers owe winners swing mowing twice

pr ec ta 6 Take practice seriously because correct keying can be attainable.
pr ec ta 7 praise apron pro press echo deck spec beech talk notary stay beta

ra si ri 8 Chasing rainbows and the thrill of singing in the rain is daring.
ra si ri 9 raid mirage algebra sign desire music crisp ripe drip basic drill

6c ACCURACY BUILDER

Directions Key from the software screen. You will have three attempts to key each sentence within the accuracy limits.

10 We do appreciate your letter and know you will enjoy the musical.
11 With your permission, we would like to add your name to our list.
12 I am sure you are aware that we would really like to be included.

Press On

Good Job! You have finished the first set of speed lessons and now you are facing the accuracy challenge. No simple procedure or fix eliminates errors. Errors are best managed by reducing stress and striving to key at a controlled rate. To key accurately, key at a comfortable rate–below your highest speed.

"Striving for excellence motivates you; striving for perfection is demoralizing."

Harriet Braiker

12

	gwam	3'	5'

There are many opportunities for jobs in the physical fitness industry. The first step for many people is to be a fitness instructor in a fitness center or program. A genuine interest in the field as well as evidence of a personal commitment to good fitness are frequently the major things needed to land a job as a fitness instructor.

Another opportunity in the fitness industry is to become a strength coach for an athletic team. This person works to make the team members fit and strong at the same time the athletic coach works to maximize their skills. A college degree in physical education or a related field is usually needed for this kind of job.

Others in the fitness field often get a job in a big company or hospital as a fitness program director. These directors run programs that improve the fitness and overall health of the people who work in the hospital or company. Directors usually need a college degree and a lot of training in fitness skills, health promotion, and business.

gwam 3'/5'
4 2 43
8 5 45
13 8 48
17 10 51
22 13 53
23 14 54
26 16 56
31 19 59
35 21 61
40 24 64
44 26 67
48 29 69
52 31 72
57 34 74
61 37 77
66 39 79
67 40 80

13

	gwam	3'	5'

A great deal of research has been done to determine why individuals remember certain advertisements but do not remember others. Basically, research suggests that advertisements first must get people's attention. This may not be so easy. If you have been looking for a good set of golf clubs and you see an advertisement in the newspaper for a particular set of golf clubs, you may stop to read the ad. On the other hand, if you are looking for a new automobile, chances are you will pass right over the advertisement for golf clubs. Scientists explain this by saying that individuals have to be primed, or made ready, for a message in order to pay attention to it.

Once an ad gets attention, it then must convey a message. In order to convey a message, it needs to be clear, easy to understand, and easy to remember. The advertisement should also focus on the product–the characteristics and images that are quite likely to appeal to the market it is trying to reach. Developing a message that best summarizes the advantage of a product is not easy; however, the success of a product may well rest on the message that is projected.

gwam 3'/5'
4 2 48
9 5 51
13 8 53
17 10 56
22 13 59
26 16 61
30 18 64
35 21 66
39 24 69
44 26 72
45 27 72
49 29 75
53 32 77
57 34 80
61 37 82
66 40 85
70 42 88
74 45 90
76 46 91

6d 1' ACCURACY WRITING

E

Directions
1. Take a 1' timing; key from the textbook. If you finish before time is up, begin again.
2. Take three additional timings, keying from the software screen. Follow the directions in the software. The software will challenge you to either increase speed or accuracy.

	gwam	1'

Late in the past century, the Internet came to life. It | 12

linked computers from all over the world to form a new way to do | 25

business. It also gave a new way for offices to be in touch within | 38

an office and with each other around the world. The new mode was | 51

named e-mail. A high percent of all business is done by the use of | 65

e-mail, and its use has moved into homes, into schools, and into | 78

the public in general. People have found that they can send a note | 92

by e-mail much faster than they can by first class mail. They can | 105

even attach documents to e-mail. | 111

1' | 1 | 2 | 3 | 4 | 5 | 6 | 7 | 8 | 9 | 10 | 11 | 12 | 13 |

6e SUSTAINED WRITING

E

Directions
1. Key a 2' writing, beginning with paragraph 1. Key from the textbook.
2. Key another 2' writing, beginning with paragraph 2. If you finish before time is up, start over with paragraph 1. Key from the textbook.
3. Key a 3' writing on the entire writing. If you finish before time is up, start over with paragraph 1.
Goal Try to maintain your average 2' *gwam* for 3'.

	gwam	3'

Every size and type of firm needs to have workers who have | 4

computer skills. The odds that you will find a good job right away | 8

will go up if you have such skills. In fact, employers want to | 13

know how willing you are to learn new programs and to keep up to | 17

date with the skills you learn. If you would ask most business | 21

leaders, they would tell you that these skills really are quite a | 26

basic need for almost all of their workers. So to get a better | 30

chance of gaining entry to a firm that you like, you should extend | 34

your computer skills as much as possible. | 37

Let us suppose you do get the job. You must learn their way | 41

of doing the work. Show that you really want to be a part of the | 46

organization. Only then can you offer a new idea. Be cautious; | 50

even if a change will improve how work is done, it may cause resis- | 54

tance from other employees and can zap the idea. However, don't be | 59

afraid to offer ideas for improvement in a positive manner. One | 63

other thing to remember is that if you want to quickly move up in | 68

your job, work closely with your boss when developing a new idea. | 72

She is the one you will need on your side when the next promotion | 77

comes around. | 77

3' | 1 | 2 | 3 | 4 |

10

Who is a creative person? Many people think creative people are born that way. If a person really wants to, she or he can increase her or his creative abilities. To do so requires challenging the status quo. A high percentage of what every person does is routine work. Routine work is done in the same way over and over. Habits are formed by doing the same thing repeatedly; they are not easily changed because they become very comfortable.

The first step in becoming more creative is analyzing the mental locks that inhibit creativity. Most people have been conditioned to be practical or to use judgment and not to be foolish. The next step is to overcome those mental locks and dare to be different. When the telephone was invented, most people could not envision any practical use for it. Today, most people cannot imagine what it would be like not to have a telephone. The third step is to generate as many ideas as possible. People quickly throw out some of their clever ideas because they do not seem to be realistic. If an idea is not practical for one situation, think how it might be used in other circumstances.

		3' 5'
		4 2 48
		8 5 50
		13 8 53
		17 10 56
		22 13 58
		26 16 61
		30 18 63
		34 20 66
		38 23 68
		42 25 71
		47 28 74
		51 31 76
		56 33 79
		60 36 82
		65 39 84
		69 41 87
		73 44 89
		76 45 91

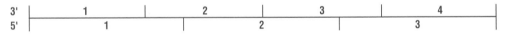

3' | 1 | 2 | 3 | 4 |
5' | 1 | 2 | 3 |

11

Many businesspeople spend a significant amount of their time in meetings. Meetings can be very expensive and may or may not be very effective. Time and travel expenses are the major factors that influence the cost of a meeting. Each leader in charge of a meeting should be required to estimate the cost of the meeting and to attempt to assess objectively if the benefits of the meeting justify the cost of it. Meetings that cannot be justified due to the cost should be eliminated or made cost effective.

How can meetings be made more beneficial? A key step is to determine if a meeting is the best way to convey the information. A telephone call or memo may be just as effective. If a meeting is essential, then it should be planned and organized carefully to derive maximum benefit from the time invested. An agenda should be distributed prior to the meeting so that participants can be prepared for discussion. The agenda should specify the starting and ending times of the meeting as well as the time allotted for each item to be discussed. Good leadership during the meeting is also very critical.

		3' 5'
		4 2 47
		9 5 50
		13 8 52
		17 10 55
		22 13 57
		26 16 60
		30 18 63
		34 20 65
		38 23 67
		42 25 70
		47 28 73
		51 31 75
		56 33 78
		60 36 80
		64 39 83
		69 41 86
		73 44 88
		74 44 89

3' | 1 | 2 | 3 | 4 |
5' | 1 | 2 | 3 |

Accuracy Emphasis

7a Warmup

Directions Key each line twice from the textbook. Strive for accuracy the first time and try to improve your speed or fluency the second time.

alphabet 1 Jackie's squad thought Arantxa Lopez was a very fine team member.

fig/sym 2 The 10% tax ($278.65) was paid "in full" by check dated 12/30/07.

accuracy 3 He kindly offered to kick our kites off the roof of the old fort.

Key Point	Keep hands quiet; keep fingers curved and upright to attain your best speed.

7b TECHNIQUE BUILDER

Directions Key from the software screen. Additional practice lines will display if you do not meet your accuracy goal. Key accurately.

nc ee ns 4 Once the concert opens this week teen fans will do much cheering.

nc ee ns 5 bench dances once chances eel been decrees answer consigns sensor

ho ac ct 6 Actually, the hot homemade pies are the object of our attraction.

ho ac ct 7 hog choice who accept backs face actions contacts conduct correct

di rs la 8 Dinners at lavish affairs can last much too long for some diners.

di rs la 9 diet dishes audio corsage version bears yours lakes alarm formula

Key Point	Your second and third fingers are weaker than your first fingers; however, they control fewer keys. This drill consists of many words involving those fingers in order to develop their flexibility.

7c ACCURACY BUILDER

Directions Key from the software screen. You will have three attempts to key each sentence within the accuracy limits.

10 Several persons made errors in the orders they placed in advance.

11 She called off her vacation by car because of new medical advice.

12 Please carry that card as a receipt that the cargo was delivered.

8

		gwam	3'	5'

If you choose to succeed as an entrepreneur, a skill you must | 4 | 2 | 44
acquire is the ability to ask questions effectively. Asking ques- | 8 | 5 | 46
tions that produce the desired results is both an art and a sci- | 13 | 8 | 49
ence. You can master the science of asking questions by analyzing | 17 | 10 | 52
each situation and learning to pose the right type of question. | 21 | 13 | 54
The art of asking questions involves the way you pose questions | 26 | 15 | 57
rather than what you ask. If you are not diplomatic, you may make | 30 | 18 | 59
the other person defensive. | 32 | 19 | 61

Most of the information you seek from others is either fact or | 36 | 22 | 63
opinion. Factual questions are easy to ask, and they rarely pro- | 41 | 24 | 66
duce emotional reactions. Questions of opinion may be just the op- | 45 | 27 | 68
posite. They are hard to ask, and they may produce emotional reac- | 49 | 30 | 71
tions. Closed-ended questions are excellent when seeking facts be- | 54 | 32 | 74
cause they get the facts quickly and they enable you to control the | 58 | 35 | 76
kind of answers you get. Open-ended questions are best when seek- | 63 | 38 | 79
ing opinion because they let the respondent give the kind of an- | 67 | 40 | 81
swers he or she wants to give. | 69 | 41 | 83

| 3' | | 1 | | 2 | | 3 | | 4 | |
| 5' | | | 1 | | | 2 | | | 3 | |

9

		gwam	3'	5'

Most people consider an office a safe place of employment, and | 4 | 3 | 43
generally offices are safe. However, an office can have some haz- | 9 | 5 | 46
ards, and accidents do happen in offices. Usually, accidents in an | 13 | 8 | 48
office can be prevented by using common sense and paying a little | 17 | 10 | 51
extra attention to detail. The most frequent accidents are small | 22 | 13 | 54
cuts from paper. Other ways in which an individual can get hurt | 26 | 16 | 56
are to slip on a wet floor, fall over an object, or fall off of a | 31 | 18 | 59
chair or stepstool. | 32 | 19 | 60

Office workers can also be victims of crime. Theft is one of | 36 | 22 | 62
the most common crimes in the office. The things that are taken | 40 | 24 | 65
most often are money, clothes, and office supplies. More serious | 45 | 27 | 67
crimes involving bodily harm can also occur in offices. Many compa- | 49 | 30 | 70
nies use security guards to protect workers and property. Another | 54 | 32 | 73
way to prevent crime in offices is to limit access to the offices. | 58 | 35 | 75
Visitors must sign in and receive badges before they can go into | 62 | 37 | 78
the office area. In some cases, workers are asked to wear badges | 67 | 40 | 81
as well. | 67 | 40 | 81

| 3' | | 1 | | 2 | | 3 | | 4 | |
| 5' | | | 1 | | | 2 | | | 3 | |

7d 1' ACCURACY WRITING

E

Directions
1. Take a 1' timing; key from the textbook. If you finish before time is up, begin again.
2. Take three additional timings, keying from the software screen. Follow the directions in the software. The software will challenge you to either increase speed or accuracy.

	gwam	1'

There is a new danger on the freeways of our country. Have	12
you ever been going along and cars seem to slow down for no clear	25
reason? In most cases, people are driving and talking on their	38
cell phones. Trying to be safe, they slow down. Also, they tend	51
to think more about the call than their car. They have no idea	64
that the reduced speed causes the car ten cars back to head for the	78
berm. It would be a lot better if the call were taken at the side	91
of the road instead of being the cause of a problem ten cars back.	105

1' | 1 | 2 | 3 | 4 | 5 | 6 | 7 | 8 | 9 | 10 | 11 | 12 | 13 |

7e SUSTAINED WRITING

E

Directions
1. Key a 2' writing, beginning with paragraph 1. Key from the textbook.
2. Key another 2' writing, beginning with paragraph 2. If you finish before time is up, start over with paragraph 1. Key from the textbook.
3. Key a 3' writing on the entire writing. If you finish before time is up, start over with paragraph 1.
Goal Try to maintain your average 2' *gwam* for 3'.

	gwam	3'

Luck comes about for those who have prepared for it. Think	4
about what you need to do to be where you want to be in five or	8
even ten years from now. What will it take? Will it take more	13
education, more money, or simply more experience? Seize upon a	17
major goal and then work through a series of minor goals to get	21
there. You must be able to know what success looks like as you	25
pass through each of the smaller goals to conquer your main goal.	30
If you do it well, people will think it was all luck.	33
If you get a job and discover it is not allowing you to reach	38
your goal, then look for other work. Do not waste your time work-	42
ing in the wrong place for you. It is up to you to make the cor-	46
rect decision that will keep you on the right track. You must be	51
patient and persistent in your quest to get where you want to go.	55
Know where your best talents can be maximized. Be sure of where	59
you are going and be in touch with those who can help you get	63
there. Luck happens to those who have prepared for it.	67

3' | 1 | 2 | 3 | 4 |

6

It has been said that human intelligence is the ability to ac- 12
quire and retain knowledge and will permit a person, based on her 25
or his past experience, to respond quickly and with success to new 39
and different occasions and situations. And that's right. But in- 52
telligence is also the ability to use mental power and good judg- 65
ment–what some people call plain common sense–to recognize prob- 78
lems and work to find proper solutions for them. It is, in other 91
words, the exciting force that moves our minds and bodies from 104
place to place, sometimes like game-board pieces. 113

1' | 1 | 2 | 3 | 4 | 5 | 6 | 7 | 8 | 9 | 10 | 11 | 12 | 13 |

7

	3'	5'
Our search for success assumes a more serious aspect when we	4	2 43
study the factors that measure it. After all, if success is the	8	5 45
end of a career path upon which we have embarked, then we certainly	13	8 48
should know when we finally have arrived there. How can we recog-	17	10 51
nize success? Where will we ultimately find this phenomenon?	21	13 53
How about a fine job and a large, expensive apartment? Add a	26	15 56
shiny new auto, a lakefront home–and a boat, too. But wait a min-	30	18 58
ute. These things show quantity, but not necessarily quality. If,	34	21 61
for instance, a job is truly to identify success, then how much	39	23 64
pecking order should the job have? How many square feet measure a	43	26 66
successful office?	44	27 67
Success is more readily found when we view our goals in terms	49	29 70
of personal ideals instead of social achievements. Success has no	53	32 72
precise measuring stick, so each and every person has to manufac-	57	34 75
ture one. If we think of success in terms of personal satisfac-	62	37 77
tion, terms each of us can recognize and enjoy, our search for suc-	66	40 80
cess can be a success.	67	40 81

3' | 1 | 2 | 3 | 4 |
5' | 1 | 2 | 3 |

8a Warmup

Directions Key each line twice from the textbook. Strive for accuracy the first time and try to improve your speed or fluency the second time.

alphabet 1 If he is six payments overdue, Juan Vacquez may well go bankrupt.

fig/sym 2 The June 23 discount was $54 (6.7%); on August 15, $91.50 (8.4%).

accuracy 3 Toward that end, we took the time to take our annual hour's tour.

8b TECHNIQUE BUILDER

Directions Key from the software screen. Additional practice lines will display if you do not meet your accuracy goal. Key accurately.

 Key Point | Key at a controlled rate without pauses. Strive for fluency by keying the common reaches as a unit.

ss pl no 4 Please turn in your assignments no later than four o'clock today.

ss pl no 5 asset busses chess play comply staple nobody canon piano unopened

rt ly pa 6 Go to the airport and pick up a package of costly art from Paris.

rt ly pa 7 sort partial cart lying analyze fully pace topaz papa principally

ot ul lo 8 The cotton cloth could be full of new colors to match your dress.

ot ul lo 9 soothe photo mother pot pull ultra bulb foul lock gloss halo loan

8c ACCURACY BUILDER

Directions Key from the software screen. You will have three attempts to key each sentence within the accuracy limits.

10 Learn how to manage your portfolio on Thursday's radio talk show.

11 At the onset of his talk, the senior senator spoke of his defeat.

12 Any further talk may violate the prior motion to table the topic.

4

Little things do contribute a lot to success in keying. Take | 12
our work attitude, for example. It's a little thing, yet it can | 25
make quite a lot of difference. Demonstrating patience with a job | 39
or a problem, rather than pressing much too hard for a desired pay- | 52
off, often brings better results than we expected. Other little | 65
things, such as wrist and finger position, how we sit, size and lo- | 78
cation of copy, and lights, have meaning for any person who wants | 91
to key well. | 94

1' | 1 | 2 | 3 | 4 | 5 | 6 | 7 | 8 | 9 | 10 | 11 | 12 | 13 |

5

Traffic jams, deadlines, problems at work, and squabbles at | 4 | 2 | 52
home are some ways in which tension is created. When our tension | 8 | 5 | 55
is about to reach the boiling point, what do people usually tell | 13 | 8 | 57
us? In most cases, they urge us to relax. But relaxing is not al- | 17 | 10 | 60
ways easy to accomplish. We frequently think we cannot find the | 21 | 13 | 62
time for this important part of our daily activity. | 25 | 15 | 64

To understand how relaxation works for us, we must realize how | 29 | 17 | 67
the stress of contemporary existence works. People are developed | 34 | 20 | 70
for survival in a challenging world. The human body reacts to a | 38 | 23 | 72
crisis by getting ready for action. Whether we are preparing for a | 42 | 25 | 75
timed writing or for an encounter in a dark street, our muscles | 47 | 28 | 77
tighten and our blood pressure goes up. After years of this type | 51 | 31 | 80
of response, we often find it difficult to relax when we want to. | 56 | 33 | 83

Now think about the feeling that is the opposite of this tur- | 60 | 36 | 85
moil. The pulse slows down, the breath comes slowly and calmly, | 64 | 38 | 88
and the tension leaves the body. This is total relaxation. And if | 68 | 41 | 91
it sounds good, consider how good it must actually feel. Our bod- | 73 | 44 | 93
ies are already prepared to relax; it is an ability all individuals | 77 | 46 | 96
have within themselves. What we have to practice is how to use | 82 | 49 | 98
this response. | 82 | 49 | 99

3' | 1 | 2 | 3 | 4 |
5' | 1 | 2 | 3 |

8d 1' ACCURACY WRITING ↑ ↑

Directions
1. Take a 1' timing; key from the textbook. If you finish before time is up, begin again.
2. Take three additional timings, keying from the software screen. Follow the directions in the software. The software will challenge you to either increase speed or accuracy.

E

	gwam	1'
Being honest at the wrong time can cause serious problems.		12
When a person asks you if you like the food they have prepared, and		26
the food does not taste good to you, it's the wrong time to be		38
honest. If someone gives you a gift you do not want, it's the		51
wrong time to be honest. If a girl asks you if you like a dress		64
that is a color you do not like, it's the wrong time to be honest.		77
Of course, if you don't mind having the problem, go ahead and say		91
what you think. However, if you do, you may have a lonely life.		103

1' | 1 | 2 | 3 | 4 | 5 | 6 | 7 | 8 | 9 | 10 | 11 | 12 | 13 |

8e SUSTAINED WRITING

Directions
1. Key a 2' writing, beginning with paragraph 1. Key from the textbook.
2. Key another 2' writing, beginning with paragraph 2. If you finish before time is up, start over with paragraph 1. Key from the textbook.
3. Key a 3' writing on the entire writing. If you finish before time is up, start over with paragraph 1.
Goal Try to maintain your average 2' *gwam* for 3'.

E

	gwam	3'
Of all the things that you need to enhance your feeling good,		4
exercise, rest, and fresh air, none is more important to consider		9
than the kind of food that you eat each day. The mind and body		13
just cannot work without the correct supply of nutrients and energy		17
you get from food. Try to realize that it is best to have lots of		22
grains, fruits, and vegetables. Add to these good proteins and a		26
lot of water. It is the kind of food you eat, not the quantity,		31
that will matter most in the long run.		33
Often what we eat may be just the result of one or more per-		37
sonal and social situations. These may include both what we desire		42
each day and what we are used to eating because of how our food was		46
prepared when we were children. Our income, social group, new food		51
on the market, and how foods are displayed may have some effect on		55
the food choices that we make every day. Sometimes when we are		59
alone we may fix something that rates a zero for the quality of its		64
nutrients. Just remember that you are what you eat!		67

3' | 1 | 2 | 3 | 4 |

2

What characterizes an excellent team member? An excellent   12
team member understands the goals of the team and will place team   25
values above her or his individual objectives. An excellent team   38
member helps to determine the most effective way to reach the goals   52
that were set by the group and will help to make each decision that   65
affects the group. Above all, an excellent team member will sup-   78
port a decision made by the team. Each member must understand his   92
or her role and respect the roles of others. Every member of a   104
team must share in both victory and defeat.   113

1' | 1 | 2 | 3 | 4 | 5 | 6 | 7 | 8 | 9 | 10 | 11 | 12 | 13 |

3

Students, for decades, have secured part-time jobs to help pay   4 3 52
for college expenses. Today, more students are gainfully employed   9 5 54
while they are in college than ever before. Many of them are em-   13 8 57
ployed because their financial situation requires that they earn   17 10 60
money. Earnings from jobs go to pay for tuition, books, living   22 13 62
costs, and other necessities. Some work so that they can own cars   26 16 65
or buy luxury items; others seek jobs to gain skills or to build   30 18 67
their vitas. These students are aware that many organizations pre-   35 21 70
fer to hire a person who has had some type of work experience than   39 24 73
one who has had none.   41 24 74

Students often ask if the work experience has to be in exactly   45 27 76
the same field. Obviously, the more closely related the experi-   49 29 79
ence, the better it is. However, the old adage, anything beats   53 32 81
nothing, applies. Regardless of the types of jobs students have,   58 35 84
they can demonstrate that they get to work regularly and on time,   62 37 86
they have good human relations skills, they are organized and can   67 40 89
manage time effectively, and they produce good results. All of   71 42 92
these factors are very critical to employers. The bottom line is   75 45 94
that employers like to use what you have done in the past as a pre-   79 48 97
dictor of what you will do in the future.   82 49 98

3' | 1 | 2 | 3 | 4 |
5' | 1 | 2 | 3 |

LESSON 9

Accuracy Emphasis

9a Warmup

Directions Key each line twice from the textbook. Strive for accuracy the first time and try to improve your speed or fluency the second time.

alphabet 1 Jack D. Gomez is anxious about his quest to review the fine play.

fig/sym 2 Insurance policy #96-71 (for $54,000) will mature on May 3, 2008.

accuracy 3 The boy's doctor told their mother he should check their hearing.

9b TECHNIQUE BUILDER

Directions Key from the software screen. Additional practice lines will display if you do not meet your accuracy goal. Key accurately.

fi ge em 4 To find good gems, ask a gemologist to confirm their worth first.

fi ge em 5 files benefit firm gear budget badges emphatically demand academe

un po su 6 Sue was under political pressure to run for the temporary office.

un po su 7 under account begun points coupon tempo subject census consummate

av os ad 8 Dave, an avid rose gardener, adds only grade A roses to a garden.

av os ad 9 avenue endeavor favor most costs autos impose address blade bread

 Key Point In the beginning you may want to anchor your little finger on the "a" key with your left hand and the ";" key with the right hand. Soon you will know the feeling of the home position.

9c ACCURACY BUILDER

Directions Key from the software screen. You will have three attempts to key each sentence within the accuracy limits.

10 Jan and Mel work downtown but go to duck and whale world for fun.

11 Be aware that the better article is now part of a special record.

12 He declared that various people were aware of that secret defect.

Directions

1. Select **Timed Writing** from the Main menu; the **Timed Writing Selection** dialog box displays.
2. Scroll to select the desired timing. Writings from this section are named as *Writing #*; writings from the lessons are identified by exercise number (for example, *1f*). To access timings from other textbooks, use the **Locate a Timed Writing** button.
3. Click to select the length of the timing if it is different than the default.
4. Check that the Emphasis is set to Accuracy and that Text Option is set to Entire Writing. Key the entire writing. If you finish before time is up, begin again with paragraph 1.
5. Review your results;

    Navigate to see the type of errors you made.

    Click **Practice Errors** button to practice the phrases in which you made a mistake.

    Click **Timed Writing** button to repeat the same writing.
6. Timings are saved automatically. Results of the last 20 writings will be displayed on the recent Timed Writing Report as well as the best three timings at each length. Click the timing from this report to display the keystrokes and results.

1

	gwam	3'	5'
A successful organization tries to put the right employee in	4	2	51
the right job. The process of selecting employees raises many	8	5	54
questions that frequently are very perplexing. A key issue that	13	8	56
must be balanced deals with the rights of the individual who is	17	10	59
seeking a position and the rights of the organization that is hir-	21	13	61
ing a person to fill a position. Laws specify the types of infor-	26	15	64
mation that can be asked in the hiring process to ensure that bias	30	18	67
is not a factor in hiring. However, most firms do strive to be	34	21	69
fair in the hiring process. The issue that many employers struggle	39	23	72
with is how to determine who will be the right employee for a par-	43	26	74
ticular job that is available.	45	27	76
The ability to predict an individual's performance on the job	49	30	78
is very important. Assessing an individual in the hiring process	54	32	81
to determine how he or she will perform on the job, however, is a	58	35	83
very difficult task. Most techniques measure the potential or the	63	38	86
way that a person can perform, but the way a person can perform may	67	40	89
differ drastically from the way the person will perform when he or	72	43	92
she is hired. Past performance on a job may be the best measure of	76	46	94
future performance, which is why firms seek individuals with ex-	80	48	97
perience.	81	49	97

3'	1	2	3	4
5'	1	2	3	

9d 1' ACCURACY WRITING ↑ ↑

E

Directions
1. Take a 1' timing; key from the textbook. If you finish before time is up, begin again.
2. Take three additional timings, keying from the software screen. Follow the directions in the software. The software will challenge you to either increase speed or accuracy.

gwam 1'

My wife and I were sitting at a table outside a small café in 12
a strange town. When we realized no one there knew who we were, 25
and the people at home who knew us did not know where we were, we 39
felt a release of all our pressures and relaxed. So many times, we 52
had wanted to be out of the public's eye. It was a good feeling 65
for a moment; but not one we would want forever. We need people 78
who care about us around us and we want them to know where we are 91
and what we are doing, don't we? 98

1' | 1 | 2 | 3 | 4 | 5 | 6 | 7 | 8 | 9 | 10 | 11 | 12 | 13 |

9e SUSTAINED WRITING

E

Directions
1. Key a 2' writing, beginning with paragraph 1. Key from the textbook.
2. Key another 2' writing, beginning with paragraph 2. If you finish before time is up, start over with paragraph 1. Key from the textbook.
3. Key a 3' writing on the entire writing. If you finish before time is up, start over with paragraph 1.
Goal Try to maintain your average 2' *gwam* for 3'.

gwam 3'

How to care for those who are old is very much, and must con- 4
tinue to be, an object of concern for all of us. As new and better 9
medical products are found, many more people are able to live 13
longer and much more useful lives. A goal for all of us is to be 17
open to new ways to provide not only the best health care to the 21
elderly but also good housing. We also need unique ways for older 26
persons to keep their lives full of zest during their extra time, 30
such as having them tutor young children. 33

The need for funds for the programs that deal with elderly 37
problems is in the news. Quite often, the money problem is in the 41
news but little is written on how to get more. Much of the support 46
has been kept at the local level. At the local level, fewer funds 50
can be set aside for this use. To adjust for the lack of funds, 55
more people are needed to give of their time and talents. It may 59
amaze you to find out just how moving it can be to help older peo- 63
ple. Take notice because becoming an elderly person comes faster 68
than you think. 69

3' | 1 | 2 | 3 | 4 |

Part

2

Success does not depend on how you feel, but on results.

TIMED WRITINGS

LESSON 10 — Assessment

10a Warmup

Directions Key each line twice from the textbook. Strive for accuracy the first time and try to improve your speed or fluency the second time.

alphabet 1 Zane Quible's five exemplary job skills did win him a gold watch.
speed 2 Olive says she likes to watch the lights of the lively fireflies.
accuracy 3 Don't let me forget to place your letter of regret in the basket.

10b ACCURACY BUILDER

Directions Key these sentences from the software screen. You will have three attempts to key each sentence within the accuracy limits.

4 We received a certificate identifying eligibility for a dividend.
5 Perry suddenly left for Hawaii after winning last week's lottery.
6 Wash and wax the aqua wagon in the lot and we can sell it easily.

10c TIMED WRITING

Directions Key two 3' timings from the textbook. Review your errors if you made any. Complete the error diagnostic drills.

E

	gwam	3'	5'

Every one of us must deal with time management every day of our life, or at least until we retire from our last job. Our daily schedules usually will require that we get up by a certain time, that we eat by a certain time, and that we leave for school or work by a certain time. While at school or at work, we may find ourselves with another exact time schedule beyond our control.

If we are unable to manage our time, then time itself may become an extreme stress factor, which may then begin to affect our health and our judgment. Often we need only realize that our case is not unique and that the answer is a simple one. We must try to change those things over which we do have control. When those changes are made, accept that there are things over which we have no control. Learn to prepare for the time we cannot manage, be flexible, and live with it. Time is all we really have so take care of it.

gwam	3'	5'
	4	2	39
	9	5	42
	13	8	44
	17	10	47
	22	13	49
	26	15	52
	30	18	54
	34	20	57
	38	23	60
	43	26	62
	47	28	65
	52	31	67
	56	33	70
	60	36	72
	61	36	73

```
3' |___1___|___2___|___3___|___4___|
5' |_____1_____|_____2_____|_____3_____|
```

10d PACED WRITING

Directions Key the Paced Writing from the software. The software will begin at whatever level is appropriate for you. Try to reach your speed or accuracy goals.

LESSON 60   Assessment

60a   Warmup

Directions Key each line twice from the textbook. Strive for accuracy the first time and try to improve your speed or fluency the second time.

alphabet	1	Travis packed that quaint, gaudy jewel box in a small, fuzzy box.
speed	2	He is the eighth visitor to visit the new work in the art museum.
accuracy	3	Chi-luan wants to visit Niagara Falls before he returns to China.

60b   ACCURACY BUILDER

Directions Key from the software screen. You will have three attempts to key each sentence within the accuracy limits.

60c   TIMED WRITING

Directions Key two 3' timings from the textbook. Review your errors if you made any. Complete the error diagnostic drills.

A

	gwam	3'	5'

When my son said he was bored with summer, I started my favorite motivational talk. "You can be bored and add nothing to the quality of your life or you can make your life exciting and full of great experiences. You can choose anything such as climbing a mountain, riding the rapids, or flying an airplane." He quickly said he wanted the airplane experience. I was not crazy about his experience choice. Trying to change his mind, we went to the airport and took a ride in a small yellow airplane. The ride seemed endless but it did not alter his mind or determination. After completing the ground school training and just about ten hours of flight time, he was ready to solo.

3'	5'
4	2 55
8	5 57
13	8 60
17	10 62
21	13 65
26	16 68
30	18 70
35	21 73
39	23 76
43	26 78
46	27 79

The solo was quite early the following morning. My son obtained a weather report and filed his flight plan. He immediately went confidently to the waiting airplane, looked it over, and boarded. The engine started up without delay. He taxied to the runway. Just a few minutes later the airplane turned and began its trip into a beautiful clear sky. The little yellow airplane soon became very small and then was gone completely. An enormously lost feeling developed within me. I thought how crazy I was to let him do this. Ultimately, the little airplane came into view again and gently floated to the ground.

3'	5'
50	30 82
54	32 84
58	35 87
62	37 90
67	40 92
71	43 95
76	46 98
80	48 100
85	51 103
87	52 104

3'	1	2	3	4
5'	1	2	3	

60d   PACED WRITING

Directions Key the Paced Writing from the software. The software will begin at whatever level is appropriate for you. Try to reach your speed or accuracy goals.

LESSON 11 — Speed Emphasis

11a Warmup

Directions Key each line twice from the textbook. Strive for accuracy the first time and try to improve your speed or fluency the second time.

alphabet 1 By May Kip's grade will just include only the five extra quizzes.
fig/sym 2 On 2/16 G&J Photo (3450 Central) sold "tru-color" film for $7.89.
speed 3 We offered to assist the school in settling all current accounts.

11b TECHNIQUE BUILDER

Directions Key from the software screen. You will practice common letter pairs and then strive to increase your speed.
Goal Increase speed by 2 *gwam* and stay within the error limit.

11c LISTEN AND KEY

Directions Listen to the phrase, and then key it as a single unit. Key the space following a word as part of the word.
Option Key the phrases as they flash on your screen.

10 a report | a report said | a report said the | a report said the person
11 fix it | key it | men own | aid me | do own | sit or | did die | he dug | the wit
12 and the date | and the ease | and the fact | and the case | and the dates

11d SPEED SPRINTS

Directions Key from the software screen. You will have a limited time between attempts before the next timing begins. Keep focused.
Goal Strive to maintain your 15" speed on three 20" timings.

Timely Topic

Image Building

Professional image includes much more than simply dressing professionally. Image includes communicating effectively, building consensus with coworkers, and owning up to mistakes. The printed and electronic documents employees produce, the manner in which they speak on the telephone, the courtesy they extend to others all influence their professional image.

Check your image. Do you hear yourself say, "That's not my job." Is your work area hopelessly disorganized? Do you delight in hearing the latest gossip? To improve your image, ask for feedback from people who care about you and will be honest in their appraisal.
"When your image improves, your performance improves."

Zig Ziglar

© STOCKBYTE

59d 1' ACCURACY WRITING

A

Directions
1. Take a 1' timing; key from the textbook. If you finish before time is up, begin again.
2. Take three additional timings, keying from the software screen. Follow the directions in the software. The software will challenge you to either increase speed or accuracy.

gwam 1'

Sometimes at work we only talk about the things that need the 12
most improvement. Many people are quick to criticize and slow to 26
compliment others. All of this tends to make us very unhappy peo- 39
ple and to believe less in humankind. It is time to change and 51
quit allowing ourselves to be saturated by bad news. Think about 65
the positive things happening at work; look for the good things 77
that people do, and compliment them often. This will start the 90
long healing process of our exposure to negativism. 100

1' | 1 | 2 | 3 | 4 | 5 | 6 | 7 | 8 | 9 | 10 | 11 | 12 | 13 |

59e SUSTAINED WRITING

A

Directions
1. Key a 2' writing, beginning with paragraph 1. Key from the textbook.
2. Key another 2' writing, beginning with paragraph 2. Key from the textbook.
3. Key a 3' writing on the entire writing. If you finish before time is up, start over with paragraph 1.

gwam 3'

To be loyal is to have unswerving allegiance to a person to 4
whom fidelity is due. Thus, loyalty is a character trait people 8
desire in their closest friends. Individuals who possess this 13
trait make themselves available in every situation whether it be 17
during a minor problem or an actual major crisis. Ordinarily, this 21
trust does not come quickly but is developed through the years, as 26
is shown in what we say and do in responding to a friend in need of 30
true counsel. True counsel is the satisfaction of knowing the 35
loyal friend is being honest; telling you what you need to know and 39
not what you want to hear, even if it hurts. 42

Companies want a different type of loyalty, a faithful un- 46
swerving allegiance from all their employees. Excellent companies 50
try to earn that loyalty. In an attempt to get that loyalty, they 55
treat employees with respect and fairness. Employers like to be 59
assured that they are getting a day's work for a day's pay and that 64
their employees are happy on the job. We indicate our loyalty to 68
an employer by how promptly we report to work; how zealously we 72
work; how we express ourselves about the company, our supervisor, 77
and fellow workers; and our work record through the years working 81
for that company. 82

3' | 1 | 2 | 3 | 4 |

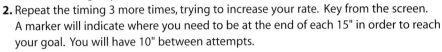

11e 1' SPEED WRITING

LA

Directions

1. Take a 1' timing; key from the textbook. If you finish before time is up, begin again.
2. Repeat the timing 3 more times, trying to increase your rate. Key from the screen. A marker will indicate where you need to be at the end of each 15" in order to reach your goal. You will have 10" between attempts.

gwam | 1'

When you are working at a computer, be sure to take short | 12
breaks. Even at work, there is a time for concentration and a time | 25
for relaxation. Each hour, walk for approximately three to five | 38
minutes. The walk will restore your body and mind and increase your | 52
daily production. To reduce any back or neck pain, sit properly | 65
with your feet on the floor. The light should not be seen on the | 78
screen. Use light that will light up only on your work copy. Time | 92
goes quickly while you are in serious thought. Before you know it, | 105
many hours can pass. Remember that your body is important too. | 118

1' | 1 | 2 | 3 | 4 | 5 | 6 | 7 | 8 | 9 | 10 | 11 | 12 | 13 |

11f SUSTAINED WRITING

LA

Directions

1. Key a 2' writing, beginning with paragraph 1. Key from the textbook.
2. Key another 2' writing, beginning with paragraph 2. If you finish before time is up, start over with paragraph 1. Key from the textbook.
3. Key a 3' writing on the entire writing. Try to maintain your average 2' rate.

gwam | 3'

To be able to use accurate words or business jargon when you | 4
speak or write is a basic quality one needs for success in general | 9
business. Through the years, many research studies have shown that | 13
skill in the use of words has an effect on the success one achieves | 18
at work. The real prize is shown in the paycheck a person gets | 22
from using excellent communication skills. Those people who are | 26
able to express their ideas clearly in both speech and in what they | 31
write will be welcome in the world of business. | 34

How well can you put into words your ideas when you speak or | 38
write? Is your word selection such that you can make yourself un- | 42
derstandable at all times? Or does a bad choice of words often | 47
give others just a fuzzy impression of the true thinking you would | 51
like to express? When you state any idea, be sure that it is per- | 55
fectly clear. If you are going to be in business for yourself, | 60
your success or failure may depend on your ability to acquire clear | 64
communication skills. If you are going to work for someone else, | 69
good word power can lead to real success. | 71

3' | 1 | 2 | 3 | 4 |

LESSON 59 — Accuracy Emphasis

59a Warmup

Directions Key each line twice from the textbook. Strive for accuracy the first time and try to improve your speed or fluency the second time.

alphabet	1	Jacqueline P. Katz made extra clothes by working hard until five.
fig/sym	2	TG&Y sold 86 table lamps at $149 each (25% discount) by 7:30 p.m.
accuracy	3	Ryan Truitt returned home for my 56th birthday party that Tuesday.

59b TECHNIQUE BUILDER

Directions Key from the software screen. Additional practice lines will display if you do not meet your accuracy goal. Key accurately.

mv oq ra	4	To circumvent a colloquy with William that is inexorable run now.
mv oq ra	5	circumvents circumventing eloquent croquets inexorable inexorably
sv xf xo	6	The oxford boxes were stacked transversely, your inexorable idea.
sv xf xo	7	transversely newsvendor boxful sixfold exonerated saxophones axon
xq xs zy	8	To see flaxseed growing on a breezy day offers an exquisite view.
xq xs zy	9	exquisitely exquisiteness flaxseeds flaxseeds frenzy glazy frizzy

 Key Point | Your ability to smoothly speed up for easy letter combinations and slow down for difficult letter combinations will determine your rhythm pattern.

59c ACCURACY BUILDER

Directions Key from the software screen. You will have three attempts to key each sentence within the accuracy limits.

10 My daughter, Steph, ran many races before she graduated from OSU.
11 I know that Uncle Chuck must have lost my recent unlisted number.
12 Bud was a Marine jet pilot during the Vietnam War in the sixties.

LESSON 12

Speed Emphasis

12a Warmup

Directions Key each line twice from the textbook. Strive for accuracy the first time and try to improve your speed or fluency the second time.

alphabet 1 Justin quickly realized what had to be given up for my excursion.

fig/sym 2 Inventory item #347-85-90 (*see footnote) was reordered on 12/26.

speed 3 Is she excited over which five solos she will sing in the series?

12b TECHNIQUE BUILDER

Directions Key from the software screen. You will practice common letter pairs and then strive to increase your speed.

Goal Increase speed by 2 *gwam* and stay within the error limit.

 Key Point | Your challenge is to attain speed on digraphs, the smallest keying elements possible. This is both a mental and physical challenge.

sh iv ni 4 shades pushed dish ivy gives receive nights clinic alumni opening

sh iv ni 5 It is nice to share opinions; it shows we are alive to new ideas.

op ld ci 6 opens topic coop older mildew world cinch dancing icing judiciary

op ld ci 7 Children open our world to appreciate exciting life developments.

na ir mp 8 names manager tuna ironed hiring chair skimp compare camp triumph

na ir mp 9 Personal and company donations amply provided for their airfares.

12c LISTEN AND KEY

Directions Listen to the phrase, and then key it as a single unit. Key the space following a word as part of the word.

Option Key the phrases as they flash on your screen.

10 the main | too soon | six pens | need all | will see | she kept | the big box

11 they work | worn sock | soap dish | big town | call off | cod fish | rush for

12 she spent many | rainy fall nights | playing bridge | with his brothers

12d SPEED SPRINTS

Directions Key from the software screen. You will have a limited time between attempts before the next timing begins. Keep focused.

Goal Strive to maintain your 15" speed on three 20" timings.

13 The element of risk is big, but she may wish to bid for the land.

balanced hand 14 May they sign a form to mend the chair and pay for half the work?

15 The rich visitor did wish to pay for the fuel for their big auto.

Directions
1. Take a 1' timing; key from the textbook. If you finish before time is up, begin again.
2. Take three additional timings, keying from the software screen. Follow the directions in the software. The software will challenge you to either increase speed or accuracy.

gwam 1'

I had an experience while teaching keyboarding at a local uni-	12
versity. I had a student keying fifty five words a minute, but she	26
had to key sixty for her job. I stood over her and could not de-	39
termine anything she was doing incorrectly. Then it struck me that	52
I could not see the amount of time used between strokes. I made a	66
machine that pulled the paper through the typewriter at a constant	79
speed to record graphically the time between the strokes. It	91
worked beautifully; she soon keyed sixty words a minute. This was	105
the beginning of the measuring of digraphs in the classroom.	117

1' | 1 | 2 | 3 | 4 | 5 | 6 | 7 | 8 | 9 | 10 | 11 | 12 | 13 |

58e SUSTAINED WRITING

Directions
1. Key a 2' writing, beginning with paragraph 1. Key from the textbook.
2. Key another 2' writing, beginning with paragraph 2. Key from the textbook.
3. Key a 3' writing on the entire writing. If you finish before time is up, start over with paragraph 1.

gwam 3'

How many people do you know who had every good intention of	4
working out regularly only to quit their exercise routine within	8
weeks after they first began? All of us surely must realize the	13
benefits to be gained from physical activity; but to stick with a	17
rigid schedule does require self-discipline and an inner drive,	21
which is much easier for some than others. Just because you quit	26
does not mean you can't start again many times until you do develop	30
the self-discipline necessary for a healthy body. Sometime during	35
your efforts to start again, guilt will step in and help establish	39
your routine. The reward is simply feeling good and knowing you	44
are doing something healthy.	45
Here are some words of advice from individuals who do work out	50
regularly. Take your time; don't expect too much too soon. Keep	54
your workout easy at first, and then add to your endurance as you	58
progress. Try to avoid getting bored. Vary your routine or per-	63
haps find something to help occupy your mind while you are going	67
through your routine. Keep it fun. Enjoy what you are doing while	72
logging your progress to show your personal gain. Some people do a	76
better job at establishing a routine by working out with a trainer.	81
Others do better working out with friends who want to establish an	85
exercise routine. Whatever makes you establish a routine, do it.	90

3' | 1 | 2 | 3 | 4 |

12e 1' SPEED WRITING

Directions
1. Take a 1' timing; key from the textbook. If you finish before time is up, begin again.
2. Repeat the timing 3 more times, trying to increase your rate. Key from the screen. A marker will indicate where you need to be at the end of each 15" in order to reach your goal. You will have 10" between attempts.

gwam 1'

In a recent survey, approximately half of all business people	12
who went on a trip to rest said they did check their e-mail and	25
voice mail often. A third said they kept their cell phones on to	38
stay in touch with their work. One in four carried a laptop. Ap-	51
parently, the new electronic era has taken something out of travel	65
designed to produce a good rest period. Some, who continued to	78
keep in touch, said contact reduced anxiety and allowed rest to oc-	91
cur. For those people, just once, leave all the electronic commu-	104
nication toys at home. Then decide again if contact with your work	117
is good for rest.	121

1' | 1 | 2 | 3 | 4 | 5 | 6 | 7 | 8 | 9 | 10 | 11 | 12 | 13 |

12f SUSTAINED WRITING

Directions
1. Key a 2' writing, beginning with paragraph 1. Key from the textbook.
2. Key another 2' writing, beginning with paragraph 2. If you finish before time is up, start over with paragraph 1. Key from the textbook.
3. Key a 3' writing on the entire writing. Try to maintain your average 2' rate.

gwam 3'

There was a panel of a dozen business leaders of both large	4
and small companies at a recent meeting. Several people on the	8
panel were asked to point out the qualities that they look for in	13
workers when their offices are under orders to cut staff. At such	17
times, administrators must make a really difficult assessment as to	22
whom to keep and whom to let go. Attitude and loyalty among work-	26
ers were listed most often by the panel as major desired traits.	30
Excitement about work and pride in one's work were also thought to	35
be vital.	35
Acting as part of a team by showing respect for those who may	40
rank above or below you on the job gets special consideration, one	44
panel member noted. Another stated that happy workers have a lot	48
of self-esteem and pass this feeling along to others. A third mem-	53
ber said that she looks for people who are flexible, willing to ac-	57
cept new ideas, and changes in work loads, yet have zeal as they	62
work toward personal growth as part of a firm. Finally, all agreed	66
that the person should show leadership qualities and the desire to	71
move up the ladder in the future.	73

3' | 1 | 2 | 3 | 4 |

Accuracy Emphasis

58a Warmup

Directions Key each line twice from the textbook. Strive for accuracy the first time and try to improve your speed or fluency the second time.

alphabet 1 Amazingly, Tex P. Bafus graduated and will quickly join the Navy.

fig/sym 2 Payment of $194.80 for a new calculator Model #2573 is due 10/26.

accuracy 3 At noon today a person will speak to senior citizens about taxes.

Key Point | Keep hands quiet; keep fingers curved and upright to attain your best speed.

58b TECHNIQUE BUILDER

Directions Key from the software screen. Additional practice lines will display if you do not meet your accuracy goal. Key accurately.

tp ml tn 4 Postpone forming this partnership until we streamline procedures.

tp ml tn 5 footprints output dustpans warmly firmly harmless catnaps fitness

kh yd yz 6 Everyday stockholders analyze the market looking for any changes.

kh yd yz 7 elkhound sinkhole bulkhead payday hydro dialyze analyzed paralyze

bn pw wf 8 It is awfully abnormal to use shopworn words over and over again.

bn pw wf 9 abnormal obnoxious upward shopworn upwind awful snowfall lawfully

Key Point | Concentrate as you key by thinking the words as you work.

58c ACCURACY BUILDER

Directions Key from the software screen. You will have three attempts to key each sentence within the accuracy limits.

10 Roy and Nan flew to Texas in June to attend the Polk County Fair.

11 Aaron called Jared and Caren in Plano about the Jaycees' Follies.

12 Canon and Henry on Broadway has now moved to North Atlantic Mall.

LESSON 13

Speed Emphasis

13a Warmup

Directions Key each line twice from the textbook. Strive for accuracy the first time and try to improve your speed or fluency the second time.

alphabet 1 Jacque's extremely lazy boys had never kept watch before tonight.

fig/sym 2 Document #45-081 (in folder D-93260) was cross-referenced on 7/1.

speed 3 A mishap forced them to abort the mission and design a new robot.

13b TECHNIQUE BUILDER

Directions Key from the software screen. You will practice common letter pairs and then strive to increase your speed.
Goal Increase speed by 2 *gwam* and stay within the error limit.

mo mi ol 4 more among memo model humid mix admire admit oleo color pool role

mo mi ol 5 A mile a minute in a school zone will make most police emotional.

im rd ay 6 impair dime grim imply word yardage hardly board may daytime clay

im rd ay 7 Imagine the impact an award has on a winning card playing player.

bl tt am 8 blast noble cable attic battery watt amend beaming dream gleaming

bl tt am 9 Girls, a diamond can cure the blues better than little old words.

13c LISTEN AND KEY

Directions Listen to the phrase, and then key it as a single unit. Key the space following a word as part of the word.
Option Key the phrases as they flash on your screen.

10 is the | is the plan | is the plan correct | is the plan he has correct

11 busy men | firm fit | pay half | body form | turn down | also sign | all week

12 she should be | in your area | on Tuesday | and she will meet | with them

13d SPEED SPRINTS

Directions Key from the software screen. You will have a limited time between attempts before the next timing begins. Keep focused.
Goal Strive to maintain your 15" speed on three 20" timings.

Key Point | The fastest and easiest words to type are balanced-hand words. Every other letter in the word is struck by a finger on the opposite hand.

13 Their field hand may go to the city to fix their ancient autobus.

balanced hand 14 Their firms may turn a small profit if they handle all the risks.

15 The widow cut the bud and may visit the chapel by the city docks.

57d 1' ACCURACY WRITING ↑ ↑

A

Directions
1. Take a 1' timing; key from the textbook. If you finish before time is up, begin again.
2. Take three additional timings, keying from the software screen. Follow the directions in the software. The software will challenge you to either increase speed or accuracy.

gwam 1'

Schools started using personal computers in the classroom in   12
the early eighties of the last century. I can remember trying to   25
learn how to program a spreadsheet; I had to learn a new vocabu-   38
lary, formulas, and other concepts that were foreign to me. It   51
wasn't until I had to teach others how to program the software that   64
I truly learned. As I learned about programming, I was reminded   77
that the best way to learn a difficult subject is to teach it.   90

1' | 1 | 2 | 3 | 4 | 5 | 6 | 7 | 8 | 9 | 10 | 11 | 12 | 13 |

57e SUSTAINED WRITING

A

Directions
1. Key a 2' writing, beginning with paragraph 1. Key from the textbook.
2. Key another 2' writing, beginning with paragraph 2. If you finish before time is up, start over with paragraph 1. Key from the textbook.
3. Key a 3' writing on the entire writing. If you finish before time is up, start over with paragraph 1.

gwam 3'

As you relax from having survived your first job interview   4
with a firm, how do you prepare for the crucial second or third in-   8
terview? First of all, keep in mind that both you and your poten-   13
tial employer will be seeking more information on which to base a   17
decision. Do your research. Your local library and university li-   21
braries are excellent resources. If you have friends who work for   26
the company they can also be a valuable source of information and a   30
potential reference the company can refer to about you. Thus,   35
should you be offered more interviews, it is vital that you gather   39
sufficient data to justify your answers to in-depth questions.   43

Phrasing, timing, and voice tone will be very important as you   48
are asked questions. Listen to those same qualities in the inter-   52
viewer. In a sense, you will be interviewing that person as much   56
as he or she will be interviewing you. Look at the person's body   61
language. Remember that about half of all communication is nonver-   65
bal. You might also want to ask these questions: What is the top   70
priority for the position? The actual specifics should help clar-   74
ify the opening. What is the management style? To increase your   78
chances for success, you do want to fit in. May I speak with sev-   83
eral of my future peers? Quizzing them will help you assess their   87
attitude and gain further insight.   89

3' | 1 | 2 | 3 | 4 |

13e 1' SPEED WRITING

Directions
1. Take a 1' timing; key from the textbook. If you finish before time is up, begin again.
2. Repeat the timing 3 more times, trying to increase your rate. Key from the screen. A marker will indicate where you need to be at the end of each 15" in order to reach your goal. You will have 10" between attempts.

gwam 1'

Each year, at the appropriate time, I have given my wife one	12
red rose for each year we have been married. There is also one	25
white rose for the coming year. I had never explained to anyone	38
the meaning of the white rose. I had also never mentioned I was	51
going to purchase the flowers; the simple arrangement just quietly	64
grew larger each year. I wasn't even sure anyone ever knew the	77
meaning of the roses. One afternoon, my wife and I decided to go	90
see our son, daughter-in-law, and new grandson. There on the table	104
was a vase with three beautiful roses; there were two red and one	117
white. Upon seeing the flowers I said, "Happy second anniversary."	131
My son smiled.	134

1' | 1 | 2 | 3 | 4 | 5 | 6 | 7 | 8 | 9 | 10 | 11 | 12 | 13 |

13f SUSTAINED WRITING

Directions
1. Key a 2' writing, beginning with paragraph 1. Key from the textbook.
2. Key another 2' writing, beginning with paragraph 2. If you finish before time is up, start over with paragraph 1. Key from the textbook.
3. Key a 3' writing on the entire writing. Try to maintain your average 2' rate.

gwam 3'

In order to make an improvement in how well you express a	4
thought, you need to realize that communication is a process of	8
sending and receiving a message. When you speak or write, you are	13
the sender. When you listen or read the message, you are the re-	17
ceiver. The answer to your message is called a response. If the	21
response does not reflect the meaning of the person sending the	25
message, there has been no clear message. The main thought of your	30
message will be quite clear if you express yourself in specific	34
rather than in just general terms.	37
The meaning of what you wish to say will also be clear if you	41
say it using few words. Surely, avoid using the same word over	45
again or repeating the same thought several times. Remember to	49
keep each sentence short. Keep on the subject and don't get off on	54
another issue. Also, try to maintain your zest with a positive	58
tone throughout your message. For example, say what you can do and	63
imply what you cannot do. In short, just keep in mind the unique-	67
ness of the person who is receiving your message.	70

3' | 1 | 2 | 3 | 4 |

LESSON 57 — Accuracy Emphasis

57a Warmup

Directions Key each line twice from the textbook. Strive for accuracy the first time and try to improve your speed or fluency the second time.

alphabet	1	May Jane serve baked quiche at the group's own fall extravaganza?
fig/sym	2	I faxed up-to-date data (in $ and %) on 3/05, 4/16, 7/9 and 8/21.
accuracy	3	Calls this week to accept my free offer suggest overall approval.

57b TECHNIQUE BUILDER

Directions Key from the software screen. Additional practice lines will display if you do not meet your accuracy goal. Key accurately.

uq uz yf	4	For finishing the puzzle he joyfully gave her a bouquet of roses.
uq uz yf	5	bouquet bouquets bouquet buzzer gauze puzzle joyful mayfly joyful

yu fm gw	6	The staffmen fixed the yuletide adornment wigwagging in the wind.
yu fm gw	7	yuletide picayune staffmen hoofmark staffmen wigwag bigwig wigwam

iy lh mc	8	There are multiyear silhouette photographs of him in an armchair.
iy lh mc	9	multiyear multiyear philharmonic schoolhouses armchairs camcorder

 Key Point | Double-letter combinations require tapping the same letter with the same finger twice. Type double letters quickly and without pauses.

57c ACCURACY BUILDER

Directions Key from the software screen. You will have three attempts to key each sentence within the accuracy limits.

10 I shall personally attend to our common need as soon as possible.
11 Judd called attention to the dollars needed for current supplies.
12 The officer will plan to send the six committee letters tomorrow.

LESSON 14

Speed Emphasis

14a Warmup

Directions Key each line twice from the textbook. Strive for accuracy the first time and try to improve your speed or fluency the second time.

alphabet	1	Kim boxed up her antique gold and bronze jeweled vase for Cicely.
fig/sym	2	Two precincts (#21 and #58) had received 679 ballots by 4:30 p.m.
speed	3	They are both aghast and alarmed by the enclosed article on fuel.

14b TECHNIQUE BUILDER

Directions Key from the software screen. You will practice common letter pairs and then strive to increase your speed.
Goal Increase speed by 2 *gwam* and stay within the error limit.

wa ab wo	4	water toward way able habit tab capable wonder teamwork two sworn
wa ab wo	5	About everybody wants to be rewarded for work that is worthwhile.
ry tu ia	6	rye crying dairy actual tube study lecture giant carriage ammonia
ry tu ia	7	It was actually a very wintry picture for both Dianna and Gloria.
id pp if	8	ideal guide afraid rapid apple copper apply puppet if lifts fifty
id pp if	9	The idea is to apply support to avoid a fall if snow is drifting.

14c LISTEN AND KEY

Directions Listen to the phrase, and then key it as a single unit. Key the space following a word as part of the word.
Option Key the phrases as they flash on your screen.

Key Point

Dictation is an external way of pacing your keying speed. The objective is to key phrases not letter by letter or word by word. Think phrases and watch your speed grow.

10	at him | in case | on edge | no fears | my fare | we joined | as only | my data
11	did she visit | did she visit the | did she visit the downtown office
12	we find | the house meets | our needs | so I sent an offer | a moment ago

14d SPEED SPRINTS

Directions Key from the software screen. You will have a limited time between attempts before the next timing begins. Keep focused.
Goal Strive to maintain your 15" speed on three 20" timings.

	13	A small panel of men may prod the city to rid us of the problems.
balanced hand	14	Their neighbor's mangy dog and lame duck slept by a box of rocks.
	15	Did the visitor fix the problems right with the vivid visual aid?

56d 1' ACCURACY WRITING ↑ ↑

A

Directions
1. Take a 1' timing; key from the textbook. If you finish before time is up, begin again.
2. Take three additional timings, keying from the software screen. Follow the directions in the software. The software will challenge you to either increase speed or accuracy.

gwam   1'

Professional American football, with its roots in rugby and	12
soccer, began in the eighteen seventies. Thus, pro football had	25
its beginning more than one hundred years ago in a rather little	38
known locale. The people of that time could not have had any idea	51
as to the enjoyment and the worldwide status the activity was to	64
reach. In a recent super bowl, the average player's annual income	78
for playing was almost one and a half million dollars. Viewership	91
for the game was thought to be as much as one hundred thirty five	104
million in the United States and one billion throughout the world.	118

1' | 1 | 2 | 3 | 4 | 5 | 6 | 7 | 8 | 9 | 10 | 11 | 12 | 13 |

56e SUSTAINED WRITING

A

Directions
1. Key a 2' writing, beginning with paragraph 1. Key from the textbook.
2. Key another 2' writing, beginning with paragraph 2. Key from the textbook.
3. Key a 3' writing on the entire writing. If you finish before time is up, start over with paragraph 1.

gwam   3'

How do you measure personal success? Is it determined by your	4
wealth, the kind of vehicle you drive, where you live, the clothes	9
you wear, the number of friends you have, the various awards dis-	13
played on your wall, or the level you have reached in your profes-	17
sion? As all of us journey through life, questions related to per-	22
sonal success serve not only as an occasional measuring stick but	26
also as an incentive to excel a little more to realize worthy goals	31
within reach. Each individual must determine what makes him or her	35
feel successful. One or all of the measurements mentioned may be	40
necessary for you to feel personal success.	42
Perhaps the key to personal success is to always have a few	46
ideal goals to shoot for and yet be cognizant of both our potential	51
and our limits as we work toward achieving those goals. For many	55
people, attaining a certain quality of life rather than material	60
gain while striving for the true balance between meeting their own	64
needs and helping others is their main goal. Some find a great	68
feeling of success through working with philanthropic societies	73
that offer such things as grants for medical research. Others find	77
personal delight and a feeling of personal success through giving	82
their time or money to charity.	84

3' | 1 | 2 | 3 | 4 |

14e 1' SPEED WRITING

Directions

1. Take a 1' timing; key from the textbook. If you finish before time is up, begin again.
2. Repeat the timing 3 more times, trying to increase your rate. Key from the screen. A marker will indicate where you need to be at the end of each 15" in order to reach your goal. You will have 10" between attempts.

gwam 1'

My beautiful wife talked me into a one-night accommodation at	12
a bed and breakfast. The owner took us to our room. She gave us	26
orders to not sleep under the top covering, but to put the covering	39
in a special place instead. We were also informed that television	53
would not be available and that coffee or hot chocolate could be	66
prepared in the kitchen until ten. After sitting in the silence of	79
our beautiful room for quite some time, I thought it would be fun	92
if I located the kitchen and put together something to drink. But	106
when I started to open the large can, a voice from behind me said,	119
"Only two scoops." My presumption is that I'm not really a bed and	133
breakfast person. I like at least three scoops. Perhaps our next	146
stay will have to be at a hotel instead of at a bed and breakfast.	159

1' | 1 | 2 | 3 | 4 | 5 | 6 | 7 | 8 | 9 | 10 | 11 | 12 | 13 |

14f SUSTAINED WRITING

Directions

1. Key a 2' writing, beginning with paragraph 1. Key from the textbook.
2. Key another 2' writing, beginning with paragraph 2. If you finish before time is up, start over with paragraph 1. Key from the textbook.
3. Key a 3' writing on the entire writing. Try to maintain your average 2' rate.

gwam 3'

College students usually can join one or more societies be-	4
tween the first and last years of education. If you should manage	8
to go to college, you may be able to join groups based on your	13
grade point average or your major or minor. As you think over what	17
is needed to become a member, you should realize what you have to	21
gain by being a member. Many of the links you make within a group	26
become lifelong links and may help you in your future life's work.	30
However, you should carefully consider the benefits against the	35
time, expenses, and work involved.	37
If you earn the right to become a member of an honor society	41
as a result of your grades, you should strongly consider joining.	46
The fact that you were a member of an honor society will look good	50
on your resume when it's time to look for a job. Do examine the	54
goals of the various professional and social clubs and consider	59
joining those groups that may increase the quality of your personal	63
growth. However, keep in mind that you will gain in proportion to	68
the amount of work you do to help reach the various goals of the	72
organizations you join.	74

3' | 1 | 2 | 3 | 4 |

LESSON 56

Accuracy Emphasis

56a Warmup

Directions Key each line twice from the textbook. Strive for accuracy the first time and try to improve your speed or fluency the second time.

alphabet 1 The big crops growing off my land quite amazed Julian K. Vexsler.
fig/sym 2 Invoice #31-76 on account #746089 was delivered on 5/27 by truck.
accuracy 3 Cecile brought many bright mums and ribbons to Bryan's gymnasium.

56b TECHNIQUE BUILDER

Directions Key from the software screen. Additional practice lines will display if you do not meet your accuracy goal. Key accurately.

fh fw gd 4 Halfway through his speech he offhandedly said we have a kingdom.
fh fw gd 5 offhand offhand offhand halfway halfway kingdoms wingding hangdog

mr mw nz 6 Movers used teamwork to make it easy to move the bronze primrose.
mr mw nz 7 comrade primrose armrest stemware teamwork bronze credenza frenzy

pk rq tz 8 No upkeep made the car's bolt torques look like a U.K. blitz hit.
pk rq tz 9 napkins upkeeps topknot parquet cirque torques blitz quartz waltz

56c ACCURACY BUILDER

Directions Key from the software screen. You will have three attempts to key each sentence within the accuracy limits.

10 Two or three weary youths were to retreat to Quito, we were told.
11 At Al Hall's garage sale, Hasaad saw a sad lass sell a gag glass.
12 Can Velez and Ruiz excavate their bauxite cavern in minimum time?

Press On

Congratulations! You have reached the final level. You are ready to make the last charge toward your keyboarding goal. Your commitment, patience, and persistence will pay off. Let this be a lifelong lesson. When you focus your energy, success happens.

"I couldn't wait for success, so I went ahead without it."

Jonathan Winters

15a Warmup

Directions Key each line twice from the textbook. Strive for accuracy the first time and try to improve your speed or fluency the second time.

alphabet 1 Jarvis was amazed how quickly excited fans ignored a parking ban.

fig/sym 2 Their newest item (#670-041) sells for $15 each; 2/$28; or 3/$39.

speed 3 A small panel of men may prod the city to rid us of the problems.

15b TECHNIQUE BUILDER

Directions Key from the software screen. You will practice common letter pairs and then strive to increase your speed.
Goal Increase speed by 2 *gwam* and stay within the error limit.

Key Point | Digraphs are any two-letter combinations. Each combination requires a different physical movement. Practicing common digraphs helps you key two-letter combinations quickly.

oo ep ap 4 book choosing igloo episode repeat keep apricots capable handicap

oo ep ap 5 When looking at a moon in depth you are apt to depict new shapes.

fe ev ag 6 feed offer life briefed ever revive levy even agency eagerly flag

fe ev ag 7 Differences between every age make a few want to vent their rage.

ke ty qu 8 keep broken cakes typed styled utility quote banquet unique quake

ke ty qu 9 Brokers like to look at equity and quality before selling a home.

15c LISTEN AND KEY

Directions Listen to the phrase, and then key it as a single unit. Key the space following a word as part of the word.
Option Key the phrases as they flash on your screen.

10 at him | in case | on edge | no fear | at best | we join | as his | my own data

11 as you | as you set | as you set it | set the | set up the | set up the box

12 the new firm | may turn a small profit | if it handles | the many risks

15d SPEED SPRINTS

Directions Key from the software screen. You will have a limited time between attempts before the next timing begins. Keep focused.
Goal Strive to maintain your 15" speed on three 20" timings.

13 May I sit with the girl by the aisle to clap for the bugle corps?

balanced hand 14 I may pay a man to cut down the giant oaks by the ancient chapel.

15 She went downtown to sign the form and the title for the autobus.

55e 1' SPEED WRITING

Directions

1. Take a 1' timing; key from the textbook. If you finish before time is up, begin again.
2. Repeat the timing 3 more times, trying to increase your rate. Key from the screen.

A

	gwam	1'
People often implement the "what-if" feature of a spreadsheet		12
to see the possible outcome of a money decision. Wouldn't it be		25
great if in living we had this kind of software for seeing the out-		39
come of our choices? For example, let us hypothesize that you		51
wanted to select between two freeways to travel on a vacation. On		65
one you would have an accident; on the other you would not. Your		78
choice would have quite different consequences.		87

1' | 1 | 2 | 3 | 4 | 5 | 6 | 7 | 8 | 9 | 10 | 11 | 12 | 13 |

55f SUSTAINED WRITING

Directions

1. Key a 2' writing, beginning with paragraph 1. Key from the textbook.
2. Key another 2' writing, beginning with paragraph 2. Key from the textbook.
3. Key a 3' writing on the entire writing. Try to maintain your average 2' rate.

A

	gwam	3'
Do you consider yourself a team player? Do you function well		4
when you are in a situation where you must work or play with oth-		8
ers? Being a leader is important, and every successful team defi-		13
nitely needs an exemplary leader. But working as part of a team		17
effectively also requires that you realize and accept the equality		21
of every person who is a member of your team. When you are a true		26
functioning team there is a synergy that develops and accomplishes		30
far more than a group of individual workers. When you are part of		35
such a team there is a euphoric feeling you will never forget, and		39
you will complete more than you ever thought possible.		43
This may mean that sometimes you may have to give up an ap-		47
proach you would like to pursue or a suggestion you would like to		51
see accepted because others on the team favor someone else's idea.		56
Keep a positive attitude and don't become a negative component of		60
the team because you don't get your way. Certainly your principal		65
concern should be to contribute to the group as best you can. It		69
is important to be patient as you listen to others. Adjust to the		74
group's objectives. Also, you must adjust your own thinking when		78
necessary, and be fully supportive of everything that amounts to		82
the group's final decision. The synergy of the group depends upon		87
your continued contributions.		89

3' | 1 | 2 | 3 | 4 |

15e 1' SPEED WRITING

Directions

1. Take a 1' timing; key from the textbook. If you finish before time is up, begin again.
2. Repeat the timing 3 more times, trying to increase your rate. Key from the screen. A marker will indicate where you need to be at the end of each 15" in order to reach your goal. You will have 10" between attempts.

gwam 1'

Reminiscences are never better than when two people meet after	13
not seeing each other for an extended period. Each is ready to	25
tell a story about an event, a place, or a mutual friend. As a	38
rule, others are around to listen to the story, but they cannot see	52
in their minds the complete picture being drawn by the two friends.	66
However, I have observed that when reminiscences go too far back or	79
are told too often, they may become a little bit inflated. To ex-	92
pand upon a story a bit is adequate; it is done for the entertain-	105
ment of others who happen to hear the story.	114

1' | 1 | 2 | 3 | 4 | 5 | 6 | 7 | 8 | 9 | 10 | 11 | 12 | 13 |

15f SUSTAINED WRITING

Directions

1. Key a 2' writing, beginning with paragraph 1. Key from the textbook.
2. Key another 2' writing, beginning with paragraph 2. If you finish before time is up, start over with paragraph 1. Key from the textbook.
3. Key a 3' writing on the entire writing. Try to maintain your average 2' rate.

gwam 3'

An important skill for every good executive to acquire is how	4
to bring about change effectively. The time to make a change is	8
probably the hardest to determine. By nature, people often resist	13
change. Employees reject change sometimes out of fear of the un-	17
known and other times because they just are happy with what exists	22
now and want to keep it that way. Others are afraid of losing	26
their position or power. A good executive can understand that this	30
situation may exist and will work to rise above it when a change is	35
best for the firm and for the employees involved.	38
A good executive will promote any change that has a positive	42
effect on his employees and benefits the company. He or she can do	47
this by following this modus operandi: First, propose the idea to	51
all who need to know by saying the change is reasonable. Next, ac-	56
quire input to help bring about the new change. Make those who	60
will be involved in the change feel they are a part of the plan.	64
Finally, after the change has been completed, examine the results	69
from time to time. Talk to those employees who made a change; ask	73
for their opinion. Above all, don't forget to praise and reassure	78
those people involved each step of the way.	81

3' | 1 | 2 | 3 | 4 |

Speed Emphasis

55a Warmup

Directions Key each line twice from the textbook. Strive for accuracy the first time and try to improve your speed or fluency the second time.

alphabet 1 LX Jacuzzi's had kept quite a system of very big underwater jets.
fig/sym 2 If your order #2964-0 of 7/5 is not received by 8/13 please call.
speed 3 I concede my Uncle Bret must have lost my recent unlisted number.

 Key Point Your challenge is to attain speed on digraphs, the smallest keying elements possible. This is both a mental and physical challenge.

55b TECHNIQUE BUILDER

Directions Key from the software screen. You will practice common letter pairs and then strive to increase your speed.
Goal Increase speed by 2 *gwam* and stay within the error limit.

ih iw mt 4 livelihood likelihood multiwall handiwork multiwave warmth dreamt
ih iw mt 5 A likelihood of warmth escaping from a multiwall facility is low.

sg uk vu 6 disgrace newsgroup disgust fluke rebuke duke divulged revue uvula
sg uk vu 7 The duke had some misgivings about divulging any new information.

wc wk dk 8 newcomers showcases awkward hawk hawks handkerchief handkerchiefs
wc wk dk 9 The newcomer failed to entice the hawk with a green handkerchief.

55c LISTEN AND KEY

Directions Listen to the phrase, and then key it as a single unit. Key the space following a word as part of the word.
Option Key the phrases as they flash on your screen.

10 promise yourself | to talk health and happiness | to every person you
11 meet; | to work for the best, | to think only the best, | and to expect
12 only the best; | to make your friends know | they are special indeed.

55d SPEED SPRINTS

Directions Key from the software screen. You will have a limited time between attempts before the next timing begins. Keep focused.
Goal Strive to maintain your 15" speed on three 20" timings.

13 Focus on the good and vivid authentic signs to find the bushbuck.
balanced hand 14 He did go on the prowl to fight with the boa, ducks, and codfish.
15 Did the visitor fix the problems right with the vivid visual aid?

LESSON 16

Accuracy Emphasis

16a Warmup

Directions Key each line twice from the textbook. Strive for accuracy the first time and try to improve your speed or fluency the second time.

alphabet 1 Jim's quartet sang better and won six of several key cash prizes.
fig/sym 2 He traded Items #891, #267, and #354 for new ones costing $1,400.
accuracy 3 The brass quartet practices extra hours while away on many tours.

16b TECHNIQUE BUILDER

Directions Key from the software screen. Additional practice lines will display if you do not meet your accuracy goal. Key accurately.

sa bo ex 4 Save four box tops and receive an extra discount on the next box.
sa bo ex 5 said usage visa sad boat labor oboe bond excel texture annex exam

bu ov ig 6 Bullfighting is very popular in Spain, providing delight for all.
bu ov ig 7 built album buy overage improves love igloo design dig overweight

uc cl gr 8 Educators clearly want students to grasp their program materials.
uc cl gr 9 auction conduct truck classes decline uncle grand degrees growing

16c ACCURACY BUILDER

Directions Key from the software screen. You will have three attempts to key each sentence within the accuracy limits.

10 The first hours on the highway are the worst for all the runners.
11 Aware of the great rate hike, several teachers were rather irate.
12 The Hopkins Hotel hosted a happy hour for all the holiday guests.

Press On

Reading and Keying

How you read copy that you are keying affects how you will respond to it. If you read at a letter-by-letter pace, you will key letter-by-letter (*slowly*). As you gain confidence, you will key words and phrases, and your rate will increase. Generally, you key at a variable rate—reading and keying familiar words and phrases more quickly than difficult combinations. Reading and keying words at varying levels of speed is a natural phenomenon of skill development.

To improve your keying speed, try the read-ahead concept: Read ahead of what you are keying.

54e 1' SPEED WRITING

Directions
1. Take a 1' timing; key from the textbook. If you finish before time is up, begin again.
2. Repeat the timing 3 more times, trying to increase your rate. Key from the screen.

gwam 1'

The cell phone is a magnificent instrument that has brought	12
communication to a different level. However, we need to know when	25
to turn it off. Turn it off when you are approaching a counter to	39
conduct business. If you receive a call while working on the com-	52
puter, stop working on the computer; give your full attention to	65
the caller. During public performances or while in a restaurant	78
your cell phone should not be on. Turn the phone off while you are	91
driving. Turn it off if your conversation would be heard by oth-	104
ers. Respect the request of an establishment to refrain from using	118
your cell phone. It has brought us into our contemporary way of	131
living; let's use it with the proper consideration.	141

1' | 1 | 2 | 3 | 4 | 5 | 6 | 7 | 8 | 9 | 10 | 11 | 12 | 13 |

54f SUSTAINED WRITING

Directions
1. Key a 2' writing, beginning with paragraph 1. Key from the textbook.
2. Key another 2' writing, beginning with paragraph 2. Key from the textbook.
3. Key a 3' writing on the entire writing. Try to maintain your average 2' rate.

gwam 3'

First impressions are vitally important in life and probably	4
never more so than when one is arriving for taking part in a job	8
interview. Upon your arrival and within just a few brief minutes	13
as the interview gets under way, an early impression is being made	17
on the individual who is sizing you up for a job; thus it is cru-	21
cial that you consider the entire procedure. That means the	26
evaluation of your apparel, posture, and the way you carry your-	30
self. If you are employed, the interviewer knows you will be rep-	34
resenting the company's image. That person knows the impression	38
you give them will be the same one you give to the public.	42
First of all, definitely arrive promptly, if not several min-	46
utes early, to allow yourself ample time to relax quietly and	50
gather your thoughts. Be careful of every aspect of your appear-	55
ance. During the interview, show an interest by being alert and	59
making eye contact. Try to be yourself; be open and honest in how	64
you answer questions; know when to listen and when you should talk;	68
and be sure to express thanks when the interview is over. First	72
impressions can be reinforced by writing a letter of appreciation	77
for the interview a couple of days later. The letter will also	81
show that you are sincerely interested in the job.	84

3' | 1 | 2 | 3 | 4 |

16d 1' ACCURACY WRITING ↑ ↑

LA

Directions
1. Take a 1' timing; key from the textbook. If you finish before time is up, begin again.
2. Take three additional timings, keying from the software screen. Follow the directions in the software. The software will challenge you to either increase speed or accuracy.

gwam 1'

There are some clothes, when put on for going out to dinner,	12
that are going to be a problem. They will guarantee a major spot	25
will appear without any exception. Even when trying extremely hard	39
to not dribble food or whatever, a major spot will appear. In most	53
other clothes you can go to a spaghetti dinner and come away very	66
clean. However, when you wear that certain brown suit, you will	79
more often than not have to remove yourself from the table to clean	92
it. The only solution may be to give the suit away. If you are	105
lucky, you may move the risk to another person.	115

1' | 1 | 2 | 3 | 4 | 5 | 6 | 7 | 8 | 9 | 10 | 11 | 12 | 13 |

16e SUSTAINED WRITING

LA

Directions
1. Key a 2' writing, beginning with paragraph 1. Key from the textbook.
2. Key another 2' writing, beginning with paragraph 2. If you finish before time is up, start over with paragraph 1. Key from the textbook.
3. Key a 3' writing on the entire writing. If you finish before time is up, start over with paragraph 1.
Goal Try to maintain your average 2' *gwam* for 3'.

gwam 3'

Do you always expect to win? Do you ever establish certain	4
goals? Do you create short and long term plans to reach specific	8
goals? Of course, you would prefer to succeed with each attempt,	13
but there is always the chance that you may not do as well as you	17
may have thought possible. Don't think too much about the loss;	22
simply learn from it and quickly move on. Investigate the factors	26
that made you lose, correct the problems, and then continue your	30
mission toward your goals. Have a strong spirit; recognize who you	35
are and where you are going.	37
When you are establishing the guidelines for reaching a spe-	41
cific goal, be extremely detailed. Keeping in mind all the factors	45
will keep you on track and will be an advantage to explain the	49
quality of your mission to others. Detail can make great things	54
come about. Learn from each success. Just be sure to look for the	58
gain and not the loss every time you fall short. Realize that you	63
must build on every success and do it better the next time. Accept	67
nothing less than the best. All things are possible.	71

3' | 1 | 2 | 3 | 4 |

LESSON 54   Speed Emphasis

54a Warmup

Directions Key each line twice from the textbook. Strive for accuracy the first time and try to improve your speed or fluency the second time.

alphabet   1   This very crazy quick brown fox jumped around scaring the people.

fig/sym   2   Sam must pay invoice #9615 before 4/30 or pay a late fee of $287.

speed   3   Did he report that they rejected all the enclosed questionnaires?

54b TECHNIQUE BUILDER

Directions Key from the software screen. You will practice common letter pairs and then strive to increase your speed.
Goal Increase speed by 2 *gwam* and stay within the error limit.

wp xu df   4   cowpokes viewpoints exultant plexus dreadful grandfathers handful

wp xu df   5   Our steadfastly held viewpoint is a luxury of living in this USA.

hp ji pc   6   mouthpieces fishponds mothproofing jingling jib upcoming cupcakes

hp ji pc   7   If you have not mothproofed your topcoat, the jig is probably up.

bp bw gb   8   subprincipal subparagraphs bobwhites cobwebs longboat springboard

bp bw gb   9   The subparagraph about the subway was the springboard for debate.

54c LISTEN AND KEY

Directions Listen to the phrase, and then key it as a single unit. Key the space following a word as part of the word.
Option Key the phrases as they flash on your screen.

10   change is not always for the best, | it does not always last, | and

11   it is not always easy to accept, | but it is always taking place; |

12   it is wise to expect change, | try it | and take what serves you well

| Key Point | Balanced-hand words help you to develop the muscle strength you need for maximum speed. |

54d SPEED SPRINTS

Directions Key from the software screen. You will have a limited time between attempts before the next timing begins. Keep focused.
Goal Strive to maintain your 15" speed on three 20" timings.

13   He takes all the news with skepticism due to the official panels.

balanced hand   14   Quantity is good if the auditor did wish to buy the formal forks.

15   The cozy flame burns on the mantle but the risk is giant for him.

LESSON 17   Accuracy Emphasis

17a Warmup

Directions Key each line twice from the textbook. Strive for accuracy the first time and try to improve your speed or fluency the second time.

alphabet 1 Vic Pugh took an excursion to Mozambique for crystals and jewels.

fig/sym 2 Terms of Invoice #57-369 (Jarmek Co., dated 4/18) are 2/10, n/30.

accuracy 3 I jumped at the chance to buy symphony tickets at minimum prices.

| Key Point | Tap the key; do not press it. Tap the key lightly with the tip of your fingers. |

17b TECHNIQUE BUILDER

Directions Key from the software screen. Additional practice lines will display if you do not meet your accuracy goal. Key accurately.

du rm ff 4 The schedule conforms to the official plans to go back to normal.

du rm ff 5 dull adult undue term conforms arm affective difference plaintiff

do ny ei 6 Many people adore their food but they don't have any weight gain.

do ny ei 7 doctor meadow tornado any nylon vinyl penny either heir receiving

ef fr sp 8 The chief spent a brief time refreshing firemen for special duty.

ef fr sp 9 effect prefer mischief frame defray refrain spacing display crisp

| Key Point | Your ability to smoothly speed up for easy letter combinations and slow down for difficult letter combinations will determine your rhythm pattern. |

17c ACCURACY BUILDER

Directions Key from the software screen. You will have three attempts to key each sentence within the accuracy limits.

10 Many fans brightly decorated the gymnasium for a musical concert.

11 Sore neck muscles prevented his attending their special ceremony.

12 The quote Asa saw was old; we should only look for newer sources.

53e 1' SPEED WRITING

Directions
1. Take a 1' timing; key from the textbook. If you finish before time is up, begin again.
2. Repeat the timing 3 more times, trying to increase your rate. Key from the screen.

A

	gwam	1'

She was the tiniest ballerina but by far the prettiest. She | 12

was so small, yet quite serious about the job of learning ballet. | 26

To learn first position was exciting for her. Time passed and her | 39

first recital was to be presented. She had three different parts | 52

at the beginning, middle, and end of the recital. This was pur- | 65

posefully planned so that all the fathers would stay for the whole | 78

dazzling performance. It also meant the mothers had to make three | 92

different costumes. Of all the recitals that followed, most of all | 105

I enjoyed seeing my tiniest ballerina perform for the first time. | 118

1' | 1 | 2 | 3 | 4 | 5 | 6 | 7 | 8 | 9 | 10 | 11 | 12 | 13 |

53f SUSTAINED WRITING

Directions
1. Key a 2' writing, beginning with paragraph 1. Key from the textbook.
2. Key another 2' writing, beginning with paragraph 2. Key from the textbook.
3. Key a 3' writing on the entire writing. Try to maintain your average 2' rate.

A

	gwam	3'

All of us appreciate people who are able to stand before a | 4

group and speak with ease. Some people may possess an instinctive | 8

ability to do this; but most people have to struggle at being able | 13

to express themselves easily, especially when it comes to deliver- | 17

ing a formal speech. Quite easily many hours of creative effort | 22

can be spent perfecting just a short presentation. Each person has | 26

his or her own style of speaking. Whatever it is, it should appear | 31

to be natural for you. Trying to sound like someone else can be | 35

obvious to the listener and harmful to the objective of your | 39

speech. The more prepared you are, the easier it will be when you | 43

stand at the podium. | 45

Every good speaker will tell you that preparation is the key | 49

to delivering a good speech and doing it seemingly with ease. Peo- | 53

ple who don't make speeches often may have to write down every word | 58

they wish to utter, but others may get by with just an outline. | 62

Practice definitely helps, whether in private in front of a mirror | 67

or with kind critics. Effective speakers also realize the impor- | 71

tance of eye contact and voice projection. The more you speak, the | 75

easier it will be, but keep in mind that the butterflies may | 80

never go away completely. | 81

3' | 1 | 2 | 3 | 4 |

17d 1' ACCURACY WRITING ↑ ↑

LA

Directions

1. Take a 1' timing; key from the textbook. If you finish before time is up, begin again.
2. Take three additional timings, keying from the software screen. Follow the directions in the software. The software will challenge you to either increase speed or accuracy.

gwam 1'

Be careful of what you ask for when you are taking a holiday	12
in a foreign country. At dinner I wanted three guitarists to sing	26
"Happy Birthday" to a special person. After trying to hum the	38
song, saying Nancy several times, and finally giving them money,	51
they eventually got the idea. They did the complete song in their	65
own language not once but quite a few times standing next to our	78
table. Now you know that to provide the song in any country once	91
does the job completely. If you sing it several more times, it	104
gets a little agonizing. So be careful of what you request in a	117
foreign country, and don't tip too much.	125

1' | 1 | 2 | 3 | 4 | 5 | 6 | 7 | 8 | 9 | 10 | 11 | 12 | 13 |

17e SUSTAINED WRITING

LA

Directions

1. Key a 2' writing, beginning with paragraph 1. Key from the textbook.
2. Key another 2' writing, beginning with paragraph 2. If you finish before time is up, start over with paragraph 1. Key from the textbook.
3. Key a 3' writing on the entire writing. If you finish before time is up, start over with paragraph 1.

Goal Try to maintain your average 2' *gwam* for 3'.

gwam 3'

We are told to exercise by health experts and often by our	4
family doctor when we are having medical problems. It is usually	8
suggested that we set aside some time each day or several times a	13
week for physical exercise. We can choose a sport; a special type	17
of exercise program such as swimming or other water activity; a	21
hobby that will generate a great deal of physical activity such as	26
growing prize flowers; or just simply quick walking. Once the	30
choice of time and type of exercise is made, the real test is to do	35
it on a regular basis. It is so easy to miss once or twice and	39
then lose interest.	40
The idea of physical exercise is to enrich our lives with the	44
pleasure of having good health. What better benefit could we have	49
than feeling at our best all the time? Research has shown that be-	53
ing active is related to having our health enhanced. Your quality	58
of life is your greatest asset. The emotional advantage of exer-	62
cise is that you feel so good for having completed the task. There	67
is no good reason for not doing exercise unless we think being lazy	71
is a fine quality. I don't think lazy is good. So just do it.	75
Exercise for your health.	77

3' | 1 | 2 | 3 | 4 |

LESSON 53 | Speed Emphasis

53a Warmup

Directions Key each line twice from the textbook. Strive for accuracy the first time and try to improve your speed or fluency the second time.

alphabet 1 J.V. said the prize for any quality work begins with extra magic.
fig/sym 2 We show 237 T-shirts (100% cotton), $9.85 each ($6.40 wholesale).
speed 3 Personal amounts discounted to customers averaged more this year.

Key Point Tap the key—do not press it. Tap it lightly with the tip of your fingers.

53b TECHNIQUE BUILDER

Directions Key from the software screen. You will practice common letter pairs and then strive to increase your speed.
Goal Increase speed by 2 *gwam* and stay within the error limit.

ao ii pd 4 chaos extraordinary chaos skiing skiing updates updrafts updating
ao ii pd 5 The extraordinary skiing update was in today's Journal newspaper.

kc pb aq 6 crankcase bookcases chipboard cupboards plaques aqueducts vaquero
kc pb aq 7 Ron please put the plaques in the bookcases, not in the cupboard.

kr kt pg 8 bankruptcies muskrat cocktails neckties stopgap upgrade upgrading
kr kt pg 9 The required upgraded blacktop caused the company to go bankrupt.

53c LISTEN AND KEY

Directions Listen to the phrase, and then key it as a single unit. Key the space following a word as part of the word.
Option Key the phrases as they flash on your screen.

10 clothes do serve a purpose; | they make a statement about a person
11 clothes should be fitting and fresh | and reflect a personality; | a
12 mirror | and a bit of common sense | will show if clothes are proper

53d SPEED SPRINTS

Directions Key from the software screen. You will have a limited time between attempts before the next timing begins. Keep focused.
Goal Strive to maintain your 15" speed on three 20" timings.

13 If he has the vigor to work he may work downtown or in the field.
balanced hand 14 He did spend the right quantity of island work on the assignment.
15 The formal proxy did make the issue audible for the student body.

LESSON 18 | Accuracy Emphasis

18a Warmup

Directions Key each line twice from the textbook. Strive for accuracy the first time and try to improve your speed or fluency the second time.

alphabet 1 Jim G. Perez lived in quiet luxury in the back of a Welsh castle.

fig/sym 2 My note (#196) for $72,580.40 is due June 30 (plus 10% interest).

accuracy 3 Based upon the outcome of the tours, I thought they were pleased.

18b TECHNIQUE BUILDER

Directions Key from the software screen. Additional practice lines will display if you do not meet your accuracy goal. Key accurately.

 Key Point | Your challenge is to attain speed on digraphs, the smallest keying elements possible. This is both a mental and physical challenge.

od da ue 4 Each day our body values the fuel we give it by the foods we eat.

od da ue 5 odd codes good dads cedar data agenda dues accrued fatigue argued

gh rn cu 6 The corn crop was calculated to be cut to roughly eighty bushels.

gh rn cu 7 ghettos caught enough yarn learn earnest turn cubic circuit incur

by fu fa 8 Fumes fanned by the winds were awful for the father and his baby.

by fu fa 9 by abyss standby funds artfully refunds facing befall alfalfa fad

18c ACCURACY BUILDER

Directions Key from the software screen. You will have three attempts to key each sentence within the accuracy limits.

10 On second thought, we do intend to join that protest again later.

11 The loud noise ought to ease later, but the first hour was rough.

12 Cedric Dickeson was elected to serve on the civic center council.

52e 1' SPEED WRITING

↑↑

Directions
1. Take a 1' timing; key from the textbook. If you finish before time is up, begin again.
2. Repeat the timing 3 more times, trying to increase your rate. Key from the screen.

A

<table>
<tr><td></td><td>gwam 1'</td></tr>
</table>

	gwam 1'
I have heard people say that red cars get more tickets than	12
cars of another color. However, I have not found any real scien-	25
tific studies that have indicated this to be true. Maybe it's all	38
psychological; just imagine a bullfight for example. The matador	51
sure seems confident with his red cape, and the bull sure feels en-	65
ticed by the red cape. People who drive red automobiles may thrive	78
on the challenge; while a law enforcement officer wants to make	91
sure they don't get away with it.	98

1' | 1 | 2 | 3 | 4 | 5 | 6 | 7 | 8 | 9 | 10 | 11 | 12 | 13 |

52f SUSTAINED WRITING

Directions
1. Key a 2' writing, beginning with paragraph 1. Key from the textbook.
2. Key another 2' writing, beginning with paragraph 2. Key from the textbook.
3. Key a 3' writing on the entire writing. Try to maintain your average 2' rate.

A

	gwam 3'
Suppose, for whatever reason, you decide to quit your job and	4
seek a position elsewhere. When do you inform your current em-	8
ployer that you are looking for another job? You must anticipate	13
your employer's reaction; some employers will think you are just	17
trying to get a pay raise or a promotion. Experts do not agree as	21
to how soon you should reveal your decision. Many recommend that	26
you wait until you have another job offer in writing before you	30
mention your intentions. Others say that ethically you should no-	34
tify your boss as early as you can. No matter what, be sure to	39
pursue the policy of the company. They deserve to know, so that	43
they can make their adjustment plans for your replacement.	47
Whether you notify your boss in advance depends upon how	51
smoothly you get along with his or her management style. Some	55
bosses may accept your decision in a positive manner; others may	59
take your leaving as implied criticism and seize the opportunity to	64
ask you to depart as readily as possible. The nature of your posi-	68
tion may also dictate how much advance notice you should give. You	73
may need to train someone else to handle your job. No matter what	77
happens, try to leave amicably, because you may have to ask for a	82
reference sometime in the future. Even if you don't personally ask	86
for a reference, interviewers may take it upon themselves to refer	91
to your previous employer.	92

3' | 1 | 2 | 3 | 4 |

18d 1' ACCURACY WRITING

Directions
1. Take a 1' timing; key from the textbook. If you finish before time is up, begin again.
2. Take three additional timings, keying from the software screen. Follow the directions in the software. The software will challenge you to either increase speed or accuracy.

gwam 1'

When buying a product, read all six sides of the box for the 12
words "Some Assembly Required." If you should find those words, 25
sound an alarm to find out how much and what kind of assembly is 38
required. Match this information with your ability. For a few 51
people this may not be a problem. However, for the vast majority 64
of people this can lead to minor problems, such as bad words or 77
small cuts. For other people, it may be a more serious problem, 90
such as leaving home. So before you buy an item that requires 103
some assembly, know your ability and your patience level. If you 116
are careful, life can be good. 122

1' | 1 | 2 | 3 | 4 | 5 | 6 | 7 | 8 | 9 | 10 | 11 | 12 | 13 |

18e SUSTAINED WRITING

Directions
1. Key a 2' writing, beginning with paragraph 1. Key from the textbook.
2. Key another 2' writing, beginning with paragraph 2. Key from the textbook.
3. Key a 3' writing on the entire writing. If you finish before time is up, start over with paragraph 1.

gwam 3'

Much of our everyday contact with people involves conversa- 4
tion. We certainly should recognize the fact that a great deal of 8
what we enjoy and how we prosper in life may well depend on our 13
ability to converse with other people. This ability to speak with 17
other people on the job or off the job is critical to success in 21
our personal and professional relationships. If we are able to 26
talk easily with people, we are more apt to know them and they will 30
know us better, too. It is important that ideas flow freely be- 34
tween two people. Try to remember that talking with any person is 39
a two-way process. 40

To improve in this skill, the most difficult part is learning 44
to remain quiet and listening to others. Listening is an art. It 49
means paying sincere attention to what is being said and then re- 53
sponding with what you truly think. You should not be trying to 57
"top" what the other person is saying to you. Give others the op- 62
portunity to express an opinion. If you are with a group of peo- 66
ple, try to think as a team member and remember to give every 70
player a chance to play. Focus your attention on people as they 74
speak and as you converse with them. Show your interest in what 79
they say before you speak. 80

3' | 1 | 2 | 3 | 4 |

Speed Emphasis

52a Warmup

Directions Key each line twice from the textbook. Strive for accuracy the first time and try to improve your speed or fluency the second time.

alphabet 1 Some people zip through quickly and just haul five rawhide boxes.

fig/sym 2 Electrical fixtures #92-2 and #47-31 go on sale 8/21 reduced 60%.

speed 3 Betty Bush babbled on about her summer break over in the Bahamas.

52b TECHNIQUE BUILDER

Directions Key from the software screen. You will practice common letter pairs and then strive to increase your speed.
Goal Increase speed by 2 *gwam* and stay within the error limit.

pw cn hq 4 shopworn upwards upwind picnicking picnics earthquake earthquakes

pw cn hq 5 There were upward of a hundred at a picnic during the earthquake.

uu bn pn 6 vacuuming continuum abnormalities thumbnails hypnotized pneumonia

uu bn pn 7 We used a vacuum cleaner to remove the abnormal dampness present.

wb wf zl 8 drawbacks rowboats newborn awful snowfall sawfish nozzle sizzling

wb wf zl 9 The cowboy was lawful but very puzzled by the sheriff's reaction.

Key Point | Dictation is an external way of pacing your keying speed. The objective is to key phrases not letter by letter or word by word. Think phrases and watch your speed grow.

52c LISTEN AND KEY

Directions Listen to the phrase, and then key it as a single unit. Key the space following a word as part of the word.
Option Key the phrases as they flash on your screen.

10 as the employer, | I do not want to hire | just one more worker; | I am

11 in search of individuals | who I can promote | and who will dazzle me

12 to get it; | who connect personal achievements | with company growth.

52d SPEED SPRINTS

Directions Key from the software screen. You will have a limited time between attempts before the next timing begins. Keep focused.
Goal Strive to maintain your 15" speed on three 20" timings.

13 She is torn and tattered but is the usual big and beautiful guan.

balanced hand 14 The goal of the amendment is to make an authentic big title sign.

15 He did spend half of the busy retreat with the corps bicycle men.

LESSON 19

Accuracy Emphasis

19a Warmup

Directions Key each line twice from the textbook. Strive for accuracy the first time and try to improve your speed or fluency the second time.

alphabet 1 V. Brick's jazz quartet won fifth place Monday night at the Roxy.
fig/sym 2 Order 65 copies of Book #90-3 at $13 each and 82 copies of #84-7.
accuracy 3 Dean and Della debated about deciding to decrease their dividend.

19b TECHNIQUE BUILDER

Directions Key from the software screen. Additional practice lines will display if you do not meet your accuracy goal. Key accurately.

 Key Point | Key at a controlled rate without pauses. Strive for fluency by keying the common reaches as a unit.

ck up oc 4 The backup for our checker game are the doctors located upstairs.
ck up oc 5 kick backing check upset coupon cup support occasion docket havoc

ga ip ew 6 The garden had beautiful striped tulips that grew at the gateway.
ga ip ew 7 again delegate began pipes multiples lips ewes renewal interviews

ua ye gi 8 The buyer usually gives way to manuals after logic fails to work.
ua ye gi 9 jaguars actual unusual dryer yearly obeyed given edging logically

19c ACCURACY BUILDER

Directions Key from the software screen. You will have three attempts to key each sentence within the accuracy limits.

10 Does Nate anticipate that water meters will be operational later?
11 In fact, the actor actually acquired talent and achieved acclaim.
12 The personnel issue was settled following three days of meetings.

51e 1' SPEED WRITING

A

Directions

1. Take a 1' timing; key from the textbook. If you finish before time is up, begin again.
2. Repeat the timing 3 more times, trying to increase your rate. Key from the screen.

	gwam 1'

Are we there yet? What parent traveling with children on vacation has not heard that question reverberating often from the back seat? To children it always appears to take an eternity to arrive at your destination. Now I am very cautious about going the legal speed limit, but when traveling with children, I yearn for two things: no police officer and a fastfood restaurant. When we discover our target restaurant, why do the children run for the play area? Coming home seems to take much less time, but I'm the one asking, "Are we home yet?"	12 25 38 51 64 78 91 104 110

1' | 1 | 2 | 3 | 4 | 5 | 6 | 7 | 8 | 9 | 10 | 11 | 12 | 13 |

51f SUSTAINED WRITING

A

Directions

1. Key a 2' writing, beginning with paragraph 1. Key from the textbook.
2. Key another 2' writing, beginning with paragraph 2. Key from the textbook.
3. Key a 3' writing on the entire writing. Try to maintain your average 2' rate.

	gwam 3'

It is not too unusual for many students to reach their junior year in college before they begin to identify one or more career choices. Since much of the academic work is quite similar for all students the first two years, they usually have a sufficient number of required courses in their curriculum to prepare them well for an entry-level position in the chosen field. This decision is critical because changes in career fields can be quite expensive. It does not mean you will lose course credits but you may be asked to take additional courses to meet new requirements. A decision made earlier, however, helps one to focus more.	4 8 13 17 22 26 31 35 40 42
How does one determine a career? A father or mother may direct a son or daughter toward a certain choice by example; while other parents may seize every opportunity to expose their children to various career choices to see what their interests are. The results of special aptitude tests may also provide insight. Part-time work during the teen years may help, too. Sometimes the circumstances of a person's life will dictate the choices available to them. To point out the one opportunity that matches your capabilities is the greatest challenge. Just remember, when it comes to a career choice, grab the brass ring when you see it.	46 51 55 60 64 68 73 77 82 85

3' | 1 | 2 | 3 | 4 |

19d 1' ACCURACY WRITING ↑↑

LA

Directions
1. Take a 1' timing; key from the textbook. If you finish before time is up, begin again.
2. Take three additional timings, keying from the software screen. Follow the directions in the software. The software will challenge you to either increase speed or accuracy.

	gwam 1'
One way to offend someone is to forget his name. I am the	12
biggest offender of all. I can be introduced to a person and if I	25
must introduce him immediately to another, I am in for trouble. I	39
have perused many books on how to remember names effectively. I	52
found the one that described association the most helpful. I	64
didn't offend people for almost a week. However, even though I	77
liked the logic of the book, I was back into forgetting names in	90
short order. Should I find a way to keep from introducing new	102
friends or should I read all the books again?	111

1' | 1 | 2 | 3 | 4 | 5 | 6 | 7 | 8 | 9 | 10 | 11 | 12 | 13 |

19e SUSTAINED WRITING

LA

Directions
1. Key a 2' writing, beginning with paragraph 1. Key from the textbook.
2. Key another 2' writing, beginning with paragraph 2. If you finish before time is up, start over with paragraph 1. Key from the textbook.
3. Key a 3' writing on the entire writing. If you finish before time is up, start over with paragraph 1.
Goal Try to maintain your average 2' *gwam* for 3'.

	gwam 3'
Have you ever thought about using some of the free time you	4
can spare each week or each month to serve as a volunteer for one	8
or more charitable groups? Every city has a need for many workers	13
who will share their time and talent on a regular basis. You can	17
serve as a volunteer doing many different things or even tasks re-	22
lated to a hobby. For example, you might be asked to teach a spe-	26
cial class, run errands, or deliver meals to shut-ins.	30
What skill or craft do you enjoy? Those interests may be in-	34
teresting to some others. Contact your local newspaper, call a	38
hospital, or make an inquiry at the local senior citizens office to	43
see where and how extra help might be needed. Sure, you may need	47
to organize your schedule so that you can help. Such use of your	51
time is certainly a labor of love. You can have the satisfaction	56
of doing work that others will value immensely. Giving money has	60
its place, but nothing is as sincere or welcome as the giving of	64
your time.	65

3' | 1 | 2 | 3 | 4 |

LESSON 51

Speed Emphasis

51a Warmup

Directions Key each line twice from the textbook. Strive for accuracy the first time and try to improve your speed or fluency the second time.

alphabet 1 The buzz at Foxx about Jim Glenn's music was spread very quickly.

fig/sym 2 We closed all 15 sections of Course #24-97 (ABC 356) by 8:30 a.m.

speed 3 Immediately after a football game, additional scuffling occurred.

51b TECHNIQUE BUILDER

Directions Key from the software screen. You will practice common letter pairs and then strive to increase your speed.
Goal Increase speed by 2 *gwam* and stay within the error limit.

51c LISTEN AND KEY

Directions Listen to the phrase, and then key it as a single unit. Key the space following a word as part of the word.
Option Key the phrases as they flash on your screen.

10 I want a job | that provides me | with enough income | to live the good

11 life | and helps me | to reach my potential; | most important, | I want a

12 job I will enjoy doing; | I can't spend a lifetime dreading Mondays

51d SPEED SPRINTS

Directions Key from the software screen. You will have a limited time between attempts before the next timing begins. Keep focused.
Goal Strive to maintain your 15" speed on three 20" timings.

© GETTY IMAGES/PHOTODISC

Timely Topic

Professional Organizations

Participating in professional organizations is important for both students and business professionals. As a member, you will have opportunities to make presentations, facilitate meetings, manage projects, meet deadlines, and improve your social skills.

If you are interested in developing leadership skills or simply looking for an organization to network with others, get involved with one of the student organizations on your campus. Phi Beta Lambda and Business Professionals of America are two examples of professional organizations for business students.

Assessment

20a Warmup

Directions Key each line twice from the textbook. Strive for accuracy the first time and try to improve your speed or fluency the second time.

alphabet 1 Amazingly, Rex P. Bafus graduated and will quickly join the Navy.

speed 2 I did ask that he explain why those listed had not been released.

accuracy 3 We were required to prepare two quarterly reports for James Porr.

20b ACCURACY BUILDER

Directions Key these sentences from the software screen. You will have three attempts to key each sentence within the accuracy limits.

4 She was pleased that most students had surpassed their last test.

5 They were quite upset two top reporters were rude to our writers.

6 Ted stated that the released data would only amplify the mistake.

20c TIMED WRITING

LA

Directions Key two 3' timings from the textbook. Review your errors if you made any. Complete the error diagnostic drills.

	gwam	3'	5'

In the early eighties, an extreme earth tremor quickly in-formed every person in the area of Mount St. Helens that it would soon be active. This activity began to happen quite often with various forces until finally the top was blown off. One would think that with all the early action to warn people of the danger, every person would have left the area. There were many who had to run for their lives. Unfortunately, some just did not make it out.

Studies by many experts since the eruption suggest that there may be a strong chance of another such event coming within a few years. Three others in this mountain range have seismic activity very similar to that of Mount St. Helens. These three were active over a hundred years ago, with one being active only a few years ago. Let us hope the people near this mountain are very quick to listen to the sound of the mountain and just move out of the area before anyone has loss of life or gets seriously hurt.

3'	4	2	41
	8	5	43
	12	7	46
	17	10	49
	21	13	51
	26	15	54
	30	18	57
	34	21	59
	39	23	62
	43	26	64
	47	28	67
	52	31	70
	56	34	72
	61	36	75
	64	39	77

3' | 1 | 2 | 3 | 4 |
5' | 1 | 2 | 3 |

20d PACED WRITING

Directions Key the Paced Writing from the software. The software will begin at whatever level is appropriate for you. Try to reach your speed or accuracy goals.

Assessment

50a Warmup

Directions Key each line twice from the textbook. Strive for accuracy the first time and try to improve your speed or fluency the second time.

alphabet 1 Jake F. Quinn studied zoology with vitality and became an expert.
speed 2 Cecilia deeded a nice piece of land in Killeen for a new edifice.
accuracy 3 Luis Vasquez spoke to six people who are anxious about the award.

50b ACCURACY BUILDER

Directions Key from the software screen. You will have three attempts to key each sentence within the accuracy limits.

50c TIMED WRITING

Directions Key two 3' timings from the textbook. Review your errors if you made any. Complete the error diagnostic drills.

	gwam	3'	5'
Safety and the quality of life in every area of the community		4	2	57
in which we live should concern everyone. But nowhere should it be		9	5	59
of more imperative interest to our security and welfare than in our		13	8	62
immediate neighborhood. When single parents or both parents in		17	10	65
many families are working, and all home occupants are away for a		22	13	67
big block of time, it creates a situation for someone to break in		26	16	70
and seize property. This is a sad commentary on our society, but		31	18	73
we have to just face the facts as they are presented; we cannot ig-		35	21	75
nore them. The days of unlocked doors have long passed. However,		39	24	78
the amount of danger to security varies according to the community.		44	26	81
There are certain extra precautions everyone should take no		48	29	83
matter what community they live in. For added security, make a		52	31	86
videotape of all of your belongings and place the tape in a safe		57	34	88
place, such as in a bank or home vault. Contact your local police		61	37	91
about marking with a special tool those items a burglar could eas-		65	39	93
ily carry off, and place special decals on your doors and in vari-		70	42	96
ous windows. You may also consider becoming involved in a		74	44	98
neighborhood watch program. Contact others on your street to take		78	47	101
part in the program so that a special warning sign may be erected.		83	50	104
As an added precaution, there are commercial security systems		87	52	106
available to watch over your home while you are gone.		90	54	108

```
3' |----1----|----2----|----3----|----4----|
5' |------1------|------2------|------3------|
```

50d PACED WRITING

Directions Key the Paced Writing from the software. The software will begin at whatever level is appropriate for you. Try to reach your speed or accuracy goals.

Speed Emphasis

21a Warmup

Directions Key each line twice from the textbook. Strive for accuracy the first time and try to improve your speed or fluency the second time.

alphabet 1 Travis packed that quaint, gaudy jewel box in a small, fuzzy bag.
fig/sym 2 Your 8/30 display ad (page 17A) read: 2 rolls/$6.50; 4 rolls/$9.
speed 3 Their work with a theme for a sorority social kept the pair busy.

21b TECHNIQUE BUILDER

Directions Key from the software screen. You will practice common letter pairs and then strive to increase your speed.
Goal Increase speed by 2 *gwam* and stay within the error limit.

21c LISTEN AND KEY

Directions Listen to the phrase, and then key it as a single unit. Key the space following a word as part of the word.
Option Key the phrases as they flash on your screen.

10 if the case | if the pool | if the fact | if it were so | if it were true
11 payment was made | payment was made by | payment was made by the crew
12 he will call | a meeting tomorrow | to discuss | these difficult issues

21d SPEED SPRINTS

Directions Key from the software screen. You will have a limited time between attempts before the next timing begins. Keep focused.
Goal Strive to maintain your 15" speed on three 20" timings.

Timely Topic

© DIGITAL VISION

A Friendly Smile

A smile is one of the most important things you can wear when you meet a person, enter a room, or make a speech. A smile not only makes you look better; it can also be heard in your voice. A nice smile can disarm a person, causing him or her to open up to you. A smile is warm and refreshing and reduces tension. This does not mean you should go down the street smiling all the time. But don't forget to smile when it is appropriate to communicate.

Directions
1. Take a 1' timing; key from the textbook. If you finish before time is up, begin again.
2. Take three additional timings, keying from the software screen. Follow the directions in the software. The software will challenge you to either increase speed or accuracy.

A

gwam 1'

Charles M. Galloway once said, "We give people the gift of our	13
willingness to see them in certain ways which they cannot see in	26
themselves." That statement is complicated; it means we give peo-	39
ple our readiness to see the better qualities in them; qualities	52
which they may not realize they have. When we apprise them of	64
their undetected qualities, it becomes a memory for life. In a	77
work environment, we are sometimes asked to give our opinion of a	90
junior person. Look for the unique character of work being per-	103
formed by that person. Once your observation is made and a special	117
undetected talent is revealed, it will be remembered for life.	129

1' | 1 | 2 | 3 | 4 | 5 | 6 | 7 | 8 | 9 | 10 | 11 | 12 | 13 |

Directions
1. Key a 2' writing, beginning with paragraph 1. Key from the textbook.
2. Key another 2' writing, beginning with paragraph 2. Key from the textbook.
3. Key a 3' writing on the entire writing. If you finish before time is up, start over with paragraph 1.

A

gwam 3'

Realizing that in the past our young people have shown quite	4
an interest in certain issues and causes, a poll consulting firm	9
took a sample of teenagers to discern in what areas they might be	13
willing to serve. Across the nation, four areas received about the	18
same number of checks by all those who took part in the sample.	22
These were the most common responses: helping the homeless, help-	26
ing the elderly, working to promote world peace, and working to	31
protect the environment. Following close behind were the effects	35
of global warming on our weather and the melting of the icecap.	39
The protection of endangered species was also checked by some.	43
Working for racial harmony, increasing women's rights, and im-	48
proving government also got checks by the teenagers. Each of these	52
areas of concern exists in our society and justly deserves volun-	56
teer effort from every age group in our populace. What better way	61
to seek a balance in what we do for ourselves and for others than	65
to serve a cause worthy of our time and our effort. The only re-	69
gret as a teacher is that the opinion sample was not used for in-	74
depth discussions in the classroom.	76

3' | 1 | 2 | 3 | 4 | |

21e 1' SPEED WRITING

Directions
1. Take a 1' timing; key from the textbook. If you finish before time is up, begin again.
2. Repeat the timing 3 more times, trying to increase your rate. Key from the screen. A marker will indicate where you need to be at the end of each 15". You will have 10" between attempts.

A

gwam 1'

People laugh in one of two ways. The first is natural and im- | 12
pulsive; it is often provoked by an excellent joke or zany situa- | 25
tion. A natural laugh also has the quality of being understood no | 38
matter where it may happen in the world. The second is a conversa- | 52
tion technique and is completely under control by the one creating | 65
the expression. When the laugh is used in normal conversation it | 78
imposes a significant level of meaning to the communication without | 92
using words. To laugh, no matter what type, provides food for the | 105
spirit and the soul. | 109

1' | 1 | 2 | 3 | 4 | 5 | 6 | 7 | 8 | 9 | 10 | 11 | 12 | 13 |

21f SUSTAINED WRITING

Directions
1. Key a 2' writing, beginning with paragraph 1. Key from the textbook.
2. Key another 2' writing, beginning with paragraph 2. If you finish before time is up, start over with paragraph 1. Then key a 3' writing on the entire writing. Try to maintain your average 2' rate.

A

gwam 3'

Today we know so much more about the quality of our world and | 4
this solar system because of our elaborate journeys into space. In | 9
the amazing field of aerospace science, excellent data have been | 13
obtained through the space shuttle missions. Studies of the sur- | 17
face of the moon alone have given us a lot of data not just about | 22
the moon but also about the earth and its beginning. One study | 26
came to the conclusion the continents of the Earth were probably in | 30
place soon after the planet was created, superseding a theory that | 35
the early planet was either moon-like or primarily water. The Hub- | 39
ble space telescope gives us a window with which to view our own | 44
sizable solar system and beyond. | 46

Few of us realize that quite a number of items on the market | 50
today were first utilized in the space program. To name just a | 54
few, satellites used to send TV signals and to expedite phone calls | 59
are simply taken for granted in this day and age. Surveys made | 63
from space of the earth and the air have made weather forecasts | 67
better and have helped us in our production of many things. Medi- | 72
cal instruments produced today arise from space medical research. | 76
They are directly beneficial to our daily medical use; one is a | 80
blood analyzer that performs eighty to one hundred chemical blood | 85
tests using a single drop of whole blood. | 87

3' | 1 | 2 | 3 | 4 |

LESSON 49

Accuracy Emphasis

49a Warmup

Directions Key each line twice from the textbook. Strive for accuracy the first time and try to improve your speed or fluency the second time.

alphabet 1 Zookeeper Bobby Jack spends quiet times with a very fragile lynx.
fig/sym 2 The theater is 100% booked for shows on 2/7, 3/19, 4/6, and 5/18.
accuracy 3 Neither brother can find the facility to house the local program.

49b TECHNIQUE BUILDER

Directions Key from the software screen. Additional practice lines will display if you do not meet your accuracy goal. Key accurately.

hf xy yn 4 You must faithfully learn the dynamics of using a plane's oxygen.
hf xy yn 5 mouthful youthful wishful oxygen xylenes proxy keynote syndicated

dh td kb 6 Bondholders thought the entry was to be outdated in the workbook.
dh td kb 7 childhood adherent redheaded shutdowns outdoor backbone stickball

lg kk wd 8 The algebra and bookkeeping classes were overcrowded each period.
lg kk wd 9 tollgates indulgence algae knickknacks lockkeepers powder sawdust

 Key Point | Because of key location and the finger you use, the actual keying time for letters varies. Do not try to type each key at the same rate.

49c ACCURACY BUILDER

Directions Key from the software screen. You will have three attempts to key each sentence within the accuracy limits.

10 Can we sanction an inferior diagram and yet acquire quality work?
11 We opted to try to pool our property prior to our trip to Europe.
12 Hal thinks Daniel has shaded glass; his dad has shaded glass too.

LESSON 22

Speed Emphasis

22a Warmup

Directions Key each line twice from the textbook. Strive for accuracy the first time and try to improve your speed or fluency the second time.

alphabet	1	May Jane serve baked quiche at the group's own fall extravaganza.
fig/sym	2	I faxed up-to-date data (in $ and %) on 3/5, 4/27, 6/9, and 8/10.
speed	3	Chances are that Chap will succeed their current committee chair.

22b TECHNIQUE BUILDER

Directions Key from the software screen. You will practice common letter pairs and then strive to increase your speed.
Goal Increase speed by 2 *gwam* and stay within the error limit.

ak ba nu	4	oak shaker peak abandon embassy urban nurses manuals manufactures
ak ba nu	5	This bakery makes banana nut bread with genuine nutritious flour.
rv mm lu	6	nervous marvels preserved comma grammar immune plus includes luck
rv mm lu	7	A survey during intervals commencing immediately gives us a clue.
rr cc rc	8	irregular mirror sorry accept succeeds accuse porch orca enforced
rr cc rc	9	Eating cherry pie can force exercise according to the specialist.

22c LISTEN AND KEY

Directions Listen to the phrase, and then key it as a single unit. Key the space following a word as part of the word.
Option Key the phrases as they flash on your screen.

10	and the date | for the address | refer to the address | give the result
11	as you see | we are only | my tax case | are you aware | as you save time
12	they will pay the team | after they help us | clean out the old house

22d SPEED SPRINTS

Directions Key from the software screen. You will have a limited time between attempts before the next timing begins. Keep focused.
Goal Strive to maintain your 15" speed on three 20" timings.

Key Point	The fastest and easiest words to type are balanced-hand words. Every other letter in the word is struck by a finger on the opposite hand.

	13	The big social goals kept the focus of the panel busy for us all.
balanced hand	14	The theory is visible and firm to the man with the eight bushels.
	15	The flame born of the chapel is apt to burn when it is kept cozy.

48d 1' ACCURACY WRITING ↑↑

A

Directions
1. Take a 1' timing; key from the textbook. If you finish before time is up, begin again.
2. Take three additional timings, keying from the software screen. Follow the directions in the software. The software will challenge you to either increase speed or accuracy.

gwam 1'

Consumers often reach for debit or credit cards. Data shows	12
that seventy six percent of American households had at least one	25
credit card at the start of this century. Plastic can have a high	39
interest rate since it requires no collateral. Consumers can get	52
into trouble if they are not careful because it is easy to misuse	65
the cards. Be sure to use only one major card, don't overspend,	78
pay your bill promptly, and don't make just the minimum payment.	91

1' | 1 | 2 | 3 | 4 | 5 | 6 | 7 | 8 | 9 | 10 | 11 | 12 | 13 |

48e SUSTAINED WRITING

A

Directions
1. Key a 2' writing, beginning with paragraph 1. Key from the textbook.
2. Key another 2' writing, beginning with paragraph 2. Key from the textbook.
3. Key a 3' writing on the entire writing. If you finish before time is up, start over with paragraph 1.

gwam 3'

So often we hear of workers changing jobs because they cannot	4
get along with their boss, supervisor, or maybe a fellow employee.	9
Working smoothly with others and adjusting to those whose character	13
traits may be quite different from our own can be more difficult	18
for some than for others. All of us usually realize early in life	22
that personality conflicts can occur on any job, and a responsible	26
worker will try to work in harmony. Harmony is very important but	31
if doing so makes your life stressful, it is time to look for a	35
transfer or new employment. Just remember to do so in a friendly	40
and responsible manner. It will help ease the transition.	44
In one specific survey, however, when top officers were asked	48
the single most common reason workers exit a firm, more than a	52
third cited "lack of praise and recognition." All of us like to be	56
told on occasion that we are doing a good job. "Compensation" came	61
in second in the survey; "limited authority" and "personality con-	65
flicts" were listed third and fourth in the poll. Some people	69
struggle along wherever they are for the sake of job security,	74
which is their prerogative. However, such sacrifices can make much	78
of your life difficult. You may also be sacrificing what you are	83
truly capable of doing.	84

3' | 1 | 2 | 3 | 4 |

22e 1' SPEED WRITING ↑ ↑

A

Directions
1. Take a 1' timing; key from the textbook. If you finish before time is up, begin again.
2. Repeat the timing 3 more times, trying to increase your rate. Key from the screen.

gwam 1'

Timing is everything when it comes to the acceptance of a par- 12
ticular idea by the public. This is quite true and often experi- 25
enced by inventors; their ideas are often twenty to thirty years 38
ahead of their time. Thus, their ideas and creations sometimes ap- 51
pear a little crazy to the general public. The electric light, 64
airplane, and the automobile must have seemed a bit crazy, if not 77
impossible, to most when they were first just words. Living on an- 90
other planet for our age seems equally impossible today. It will 104
happen when the timing is right, and what possibilities it will of- 117
fer for the people of the future can only be imagined. 128

1' | 1 | 2 | 3 | 4 | 5 | 6 | 7 | 8 | 9 | 10 | 11 | 12 | 13 |

22f SUSTAINED WRITING

A

Directions
1. Key a 2' writing, beginning with paragraph 1. Key from the textbook.
2. Key another 2' writing, beginning with paragraph 2. Key from the textbook.
3. Key a 3' writing on the entire writing. Try to maintain your average 2' rate.

gwam 3'

No country can survive without explicit law and order. When 4
people began to systematize and to interact as a group, they dis- 8
covered that an arrangement of laws was a necessity. The laws were 13
needed to help guide the group's behavior. They were absolutely 17
essential to help maintain order. If we had not established these 22
laws, we would have made little or no progress as a people. If all 26
people were to perform just as they pleased with no thought for the 31
rights and needs of other people, chaos would quickly result. We 35
would have a situation in which there would be a total lack of or- 39
ganization or control. 41

Changes in the law follow the progress of the group's develop- 45
ment as they become culturally advanced. In the course of time as 50
the group changes, invariably the laws change. Though changes in 54
society may be extremely slow, laws are altered as we attempt to 58
make our social conditions better and strive for equal justice for 63
all of our citizens. We can expect even more changes as we ponder 67
how people should behave in our society. Acceptable moral values 72
and a simple faith in each other are also a part of the progression 76
and of making laws. 77

3' | 1 | 2 | 3 | 4 |

Accuracy Emphasis

48a Warmup

Directions Key each line twice from the textbook. Strive for accuracy the first time and try to improve your speed or fluency the second time.

alphabet 1 The quality of life quiz wasn't vexing just because Kim prepared.

fig/sym 2 Tremors were noted at 7:39 & 8:25 the mornings of 4/16 and 10/18.

accuracy 3 When they mend the rug, make them rush it by air to the rug firm.

48b TECHNIQUE BUILDER

Directions Key from the software screen. Additional practice lines will display if you do not meet your accuracy goal. Key accurately.

ku ae bc 4 The subcommittee drove the black pickup to their aerobic classes.

ku ae bc 5 skull backup skunks aerating vitae larvae subclass subcontractors

dp hh dt 6 He was the hundredth grandparent withheld from joining the party.

dp hh dt 7 sandpaper standpoint handpicked bathhouse withholds breadth width

kd sd wm 8 The wisdom of markdowns at the sawmill were questionable by many.

kd sd wm 9 workday weekday breakdowns jurisdictions misdirections endowments

 Key Point | Do not practice using a metronomic stroking pattern. Let your own rhythm pattern emerge.

48c ACCURACY BUILDER

Directions Key from the software screen. You will have three attempts to key each sentence within the accuracy limits.

10 The big antique auto display is to be an attraction for visitors.

11 Raul reasoned that a rigorous routine was right for Randy Rogers.

12 Zachary dizzily zigzagged through the maze and won a fuzzy prize.

LESSON 23   Speed Emphasis

23a   Warmup

Directions   Key each line twice from the textbook. Strive for accuracy the first time and try to improve your speed or fluency the second time.

alphabet   1   Exotic park zoo guards quickly waved them by the injured females.

fig/sym   2   Model #43-26 (currently reduced 10%) will still sell for $598.75.

speed   3   That lame lamb loved the lair and made little effort to leave it.

23b   TECHNIQUE BUILDER

Directions   Key from the software screen. You will practice common letter pairs and then strive to increase your speed.
Goal   Increase speed by 2 *gwam* and stay within the error limit.

eq nk ug   4   equals frequent request inked bankers skunk buggy frugal although

eq nk ug   5   Frankly equipment equalizes the weight of huge pieces of luggage.

go bi ib   6   goal vigorous cargo billing combine rabbit legibly horrible alibi

go bi ib   7   The blue gown exhibited golden threads used to make a big ribbon.

ki ub mu   8   kinds thinking ski ubiquity subway tub multiply commute immunized

ki ub mu   9   The homemaking skill is doubly stimulating for many suburbanites.

23c   LISTEN AND KEY

Directions   Listen to the phrase, and then key it as a single unit. Key the space following a word as part of the word.
Option   Key the phrases as they flash on your screen.

Key Point   Dictation is an external way of pacing your keying speed. The objective is to key phrases not letter by letter or word by word. Think phrases and watch your speed grow.

10   after tax | were you only | my address | small decrease | decrease by one

11   pay them | when they | pay them when they work | when they work a shift

12   they quit | over real safety issues | regarding boxcars | on the trains

---

23d   SPEED SPRINTS

Directions   Key from the software screen. You will have a limited time between attempts before the next timing begins. Keep focused.
Goal   Strive to maintain your 15" speed on three 20" timings.

13   The giant furry dog kept with the busy girl for a downtown visit.

balanced hand   14   She is downtown at the bicycle docks to lend a hand to the panel.

15   The widow works on the big formal sign for the spa she may visit.

47d 1' ACCURACY WRITING

Directions
1. Take a 1' timing; key from the textbook. If you finish before time is up, begin again.
2. Take three additional timings, keying from the software screen. Follow the directions in the software. The software will challenge you to either increase speed or accuracy.

A

gwam   1'

Most people at one time or another find themselves in an air-	12
port waiting for bad weather to pass or a repair to be made. If	25
this happens, don't waste time. Catch up on your writing to rela-	38
tives or close friends with a handwritten letter. Exercise by tak-	51
ing walks throughout the airport terminal; many large airports of-	63
fer very good exercise equipment rooms, too. If you know it's go-	75
ing to be a particularly long wait time, take a trip into town and	89
travel around the city.	93

1' | 1 | 2 | 3 | 4 | 5 | 6 | 7 | 8 | 9 | 10 | 11 | 12 | 13 |

47e SUSTAINED WRITING

Directions
1. Key a 2' writing, beginning with paragraph 1. Key from the textbook.
2. Key another 2' writing, beginning with paragraph 2. Key from the textbook.
3. Key a 3' writing on the entire writing. If you finish before time is up, start over with paragraph 1.

A

gwam   3'

A number of people often resolve to lose weight with good in-	4
tentions. Some people on their own go for a diet plan and simply	8
walk in a park or mall regularly. For those who do not have the	13
discipline to exercise on their own, an exercise club may be just	17
the ticket. A club can offer expensive exercise equipment not oth-	22
erwise available. Clubs also offer people a more organized plan	26
with a trainer to guide them during their weight loss. Conse-	30
quently, many opt to inquire about club facilities available near	34
their home or workplace.	36
Before joining an exercise club, however, ask yourself the	40
following questions: Does the distance to the location justify the	44
time you will spend going there and how much will you be spending	49
for gasoline? Is the facility open when you prefer to work out,	53
and how crowded will it be in the time slot? How capable are the	58
trainers who will coach you until you can proceed on your own? Is	62
the equipment always kept in good working order? Do they have a	66
sizable swimming pool, whirlpool, or sauna available; and are they	71
kept clean? Do they have separate rates for different areas of	75
use, such as just for swimming? Do they offer competitive rates?	79

3' | 1 | 2 | 3 | 4 |

23e 1' SPEED WRITING

Directions
1. Take a 1' timing; key from the textbook. If you finish before time is up, begin again.
2. Repeat the timing 3 more times, trying to increase your rate. Key from the screen.

A

| | *gwam* | 1' |

You can let life happen to you or you can accomplish what is   12
necessary to place yourself in the desired circumstances. When ad-   25
versity happens, let your voice be heard loud and clear. Don't be   39
ready to accept everything thrown at you in your lifetime as some-   52
thing beyond your absolute control. Accept harmful situations only   65
when you have done everything in your power to generate revolution   79
within the existing conditions. There are times when you can't   92
quite make the transformations desired; nevertheless, don't let all   105
of life just happen to you. Do your utmost to make life what you   118
want it to be. You have only one opportunity at all of life; make   132
it a pleasant one.   135

1' | 1 | 2 | 3 | 4 | 5 | 6 | 7 | 8 | 9 | 10 | 11 | 12 | 13 |

23f SUSTAINED WRITING

Directions
1. Key a 2' writing, beginning with paragraph 1. Key from the textbook.
2. Key another 2' writing, beginning with paragraph 2. Key from the textbook.
3. Key a 3' writing on the entire writing. Try to maintain your average 2' rate.

A

| | *gwam* | 3' |

You will find that maintaining a learning attitude is essen-   4
tial for you to lead a rich and full work life. In other words,   8
you must remain alert to every chance to grow in your job, whether   13
offered by the company or studying on your own. Many large firms   17
recognize the need for additional training for their employees,   21
quite often as the result of updated knowledge or technology within   26
the business's specialization. Such firms need workers who are ea-   30
ger to learn about new hardware and software available that can be   35
used by the company.   36

Taking advantage of every opportunity to learn coming your way   40
is not your only task as a quality employee. Be a part of the   45
training of others. Assist with the initial training of new em-   49
ployees. You may also be tapped by superiors to explain or teach   53
them about operational changes ensuing from a new technology being   58
purchased. Be ready to share what you know with your fellow work-   62
ers. Keeping your knowledge a secret will not give you job secu-   66
rity. Sharing knowledge gives you the freedom to be promoted when   71
the opportunity occurs.   72

3' | 1 | 2 | 3 | 4 |

Accuracy Emphasis

47a Warmup

Directions Key each line twice from the textbook. Strive for accuracy the first time and try to improve your speed or fluency the second time.

alphabet 1 BJW quickly organized the cove plan for the extended three miles.

fig/sym 2 Invoice #6372-489 from Lin & Sons was for $805 less 10% discount.

accuracy 3 Ty Terry reported it is true two of your reporters tried to quit.

47b TECHNIQUE BUILDER

Directions Key from the software screen. Additional practice lines will display if you do not meet your accuracy goal. Key accurately.

yz bd hc 4 They must analyze the forthcoming report before subdividing land.

yz bd hc 5 analyzing paralyzed subdivision abdominal beachcomber forthcoming

kh tp wy 6 The lawyer postponed the stockholders' meeting until a day later.

kh tp wy 7 backhaul deckhand stockholders footprints outputs mildewy lawyers

kf ky ml 8 They were thankful that what they thought was risky was harmless.

kf ky ml 9 breakfasts frankfurters picky sky lucky firmly streamlines warmly

Key Point | Your ability to smoothly speed up for easy letter combinations and slow down for difficult letter combinations will determine your rhythm pattern.

47c ACCURACY BUILDER

Directions Key from the software screen. You will have three attempts to key each sentence within the accuracy limits.

10 Kass Dallas has a glass flask his dad had at Hajah's gala affair.

11 Roberto Jiminez brought a group of buyers by at noon on Thursday.

12 My teacher gave Hector and Jorge urgent messages from their home.

LESSON 24

Speed Emphasis

24a Warmup

Directions Key each line twice from the textbook. Strive for accuracy the first time and try to improve your speed or fluency the second time.

alphabet 1 For Zubin, open exchange would justify a quick venture in Madrid.
fig/sym 2 The new tax (.5%) did pass with 32,874 votes for; 29,610 against.
speed 3 The waiter was amused when they both ordered ragout and ambrosia.

24b TECHNIQUE BUILDER

Directions Key from the software screen. You will practice common letter pairs and then strive to increase your speed.
Goal Increase speed by 2 *gwam* and stay within the error limit.

 Key Point Digraphs are any two-letter combinations. Each combination requires a different physical movement. Practicing common digraphs helps you key two-letter combinations quickly.

pu nv nf 4 pump impulse campus invoice convey envy unfit confines inferences
pu nv nf 5 Computer input on the environmental canvass confirms the sunfish.

mb ey rk 6 embark numbers climb eye obeying beyond turkey remarked paperwork
mb ey rk 7 Ambitious people gamble money beyond the norm on unusual artwork.

tl ru pt 8 outlooks rightly subtle rugged crushed forum apt captures excerpt
tl ru pt 9 You have the option to be greatly optimistic concerning recruits.

24c LISTEN AND KEY

Directions Listen to the phrase, and then key it as a single unit. Key the space following a word as part of the word.
Option Key the phrases as they flash on your screen.

10 my dad | in my job | at my age | tax on gas | we were sad | were sad to see
11 he did the work | he did the work for them | he did the work for them
12 he was angry | they had not received | notice of the increase | in dues

24d SPEED SPRINTS

Directions Key from the software screen. You will have a limited time between attempts before the next timing begins. Keep focused.
Goal Strive to maintain your 15" speed on three 20" timings.

13 It is right for them to work and make formal bids for the turkey.
balanced hand 14 Their theory is that they may suspend their usual social rituals.
15 The handle of the hayfork is so worn it is a big problem for her.

46d 1' ACCURACY ° WRITING

A

Directions

1. Take a 1' timing; key from the textbook. If you finish before time is up, begin again.
2. Take three additional timings, keying from the software screen. Follow the directions in the software. The software will challenge you to either increase speed or accuracy.

	gwam	1'

The Chicago municipality recently placed an order for more 12
than one hundred buses with widened seats. They will be the widest 25
in the United States. The suburban bus service is adjusting to the 39
size of our current citizens. Now if the airlines look to Chicago 52
as an example, perhaps they will increase the size of their seat- 65
ing. They could even start serving food again on their longer 78
flights. Of course that might mean they would have to widen their 91
seats again in the future. 96

1' | 1 | 2 | 3 | 4 | 5 | 6 | 7 | 8 | 9 | 10 | 11 | 12 | 13 |

46e SUSTAINED WRITING

A

Directions

1. Key a 2' writing, beginning with paragraph 1. Key from the textbook.
2. Key another 2' writing, beginning with paragraph 2. Key from the textbook.
3. Key a 3' writing on the entire writing. If you finish before time is up, start over with paragraph 1.

	gwam	3'

Cars were invented over one hundred years ago. Since that 4
time, Americans have realized that owning one can become both a 8
need and a luxury. Even when there are other methods of travel, 13
people prefer to drive their own cars. A private auto does enable 17
one to have both freedom and convenience, real pluses when you take 22
into account both total travel time and the variation of daily 26
schedules. The flexibility a car offers has yet to be matched. 30
Carpooling has helped young parents who must provide transportation 35
for young children involved in sports and other activities. How- 39
ever, the luxury of being able to travel anywhere in the country 43
according to your own schedule is sacred to Americans. 47

The car has also evolved into becoming a symbol of social 51
status or identity. Changing gas prices have prompted many large- 55
car owners to adjust their thinking. Some people have come to re- 59
alize that a small car with its better gas mileage can be satisfac- 64
tory. But today the options added to small cars to increase their 68
appeal make them quite a luxury item and not always the money-sav- 73
ers they were intended to be. That aside, many people still meas- 77
ure a person by the car they drive. Also there are occupations, 81
such as real estate, that require luxury cars for space and an in- 86
dication of success. 87

3' | 1 | 2 | 3 | 4 |

24e 1' SPEED WRITING ↑ ↑

A

Directions

1. Take a 1' timing; key from the textbook. If you finish before time is up, begin again.
2. Repeat the timing 3 more times, trying to increase your rate. Key from the screen.
   A marker will indicate where you need to be at the end of each 15" in order to reach your goal.
   You will have 10" between attempts.

gwam 1'

As small children, we developed an extraordinary telephone	12
system with just two cans and a very long string. A can was at-	24
tached to each end of the string. It would be made very tight for	38
the proper transmission. The longer the string, the louder we ar-	51
ticulated the message and the tighter the string. Having to shout	64
the communication was a bug in the system we never successfully	77
corrected. You would think there would be a resolution by this	90
time. But that is not true. When the cell phone was developed,	103
the bug continued as a serious problem. I know because every time	116
people talk on a cell, they talk quite loudly, particularly when in	130
public. Possibly the string is too long or not tight enough.	142

1' | 1 | 2 | 3 | 4 | 5 | 6 | 7 | 8 | 9 | 10 | 11 | 12 | 13 |

24f SUSTAINED WRITING

A

Directions

1. Key a 2' writing, beginning with paragraph 1. Key from the textbook.
2. Key another 2' writing, beginning with paragraph 2. If you finish before time is up, start over with paragraph 1. Key from the textbook.
3. Key a 3' writing on the entire writing. Try to maintain your average 2' rate.

gwam 3'

As you prepare to work in the business world, one of the very	4
essential skills you will need to acquire is knowing how to use the	9
telephone properly. There is proper business etiquette that you	13
should know. When you communicate with people on the phone, you	17
convey an attitude about yourself, your co-workers, your job, and	22
your company. Your voice is extremely revealing. Thus, you should	26
seize every opportunity while on the phone to form the best impres-	31
sion possible of yourself and your company to your customers.	35
You can certainly have an effective telephone voice if	39
you converse with people in a pleasant manner. A low, pleasant voice	43
is really much easier to listen to than one that is loud, harsh, or	48
grating. However, even a satisfactory voice can be shot down	52
quickly with poor grammar and enunciation. Always think and talk	56
with a smile in your voice, and remember that the caller is a per-	61
son who needs your assistance. You are there for them, not the	65
other way around. Cordial speech is necessary since the person	69
cannot see your expression.	71

3' | 1 | 2 | 3 | 4 |

LESSON 46

Accuracy Emphasis

46a Warmup

Directions Key each line twice from the textbook. Strive for accuracy the first time and try to improve your speed or fluency the second time.

alphabet 1 Extensively squeezed oranges will help make pure breakfast juice.

fig/sym 2 The log showed 124,907 visitors, up 13,658 from the previous day.

accuracy 3 Jerry Wood did call off his summer trip to Walla Walla last week.

46b TECHNIQUE BUILDER

Directions Key from the software screen. Additional practice lines will display if you do not meet your accuracy goal. Key accurately.

dc oh ej 4 Broadcasters are rejoicing in Ohio for the national championship.

dc oh ej 5 wildcat grandchildren midcult gasohol oh prohibit reject prejudge

ak ba nu 6 See the breathtaking backgrounds of monuments everywhere in Rome.

ak ba nu 7 breakdowns make peaks tuba verbatim banking unusual nurse revenue

rv ux db 8 Walter interviewed for the Redbud auxiliary police officer's job.

rv ux db 9 curves marvel reserve luxury deluxe tuxedo handbag redbud standby

46c ACCURACY BUILDER

Directions Key from the software screen. You will have three attempts to key each sentence within the accuracy limits.

10 Jeff's attorney dismissed that witness following the proceedings.

11 Their accountant keeps accurate books for the annual school ball.

12 Arroyo was puzzled by the matter his class discussed before noon.

Press On

You continue to show perseverance in the skill-building process. This is evident by your willingness and eagerness to keep striving to improve your skill. Look back at where you started in Lesson 1 and where you are now. Set a goal for this level. No one knows better than you what you are capable of doing.

"Nothing in the world can take the place of persistence. Talent will not; nothing is more common than unsuccessful men with talent. Genius will not; unrewarded genius is almost a proverb. Education will not ... The slogan, 'Press on,' has solved and always will solve the problems of the human race."

Calvin Coolidge

LESSON 25

Speed Emphasis

25a Warmup

Directions Key each line twice from the textbook. Strive for accuracy the first time and try to improve your speed or fluency the second time.

alphabet 1 Cruzita may quit her job and move back up to Flagstaff next week.
fig/sym 2 We closed all 12 sections of Course #54-68 (GBA 487) by 9:30 a.m.
speed 3 She suddenly saw the slant of the sleigh as it slid off sideways.

25b TECHNIQUE BUILDER

Directions Key from the software screen. You will practice common letter pairs and then strive to increase your speed.
Goal Increase speed by 2 gwam and stay within the error limit.

ht oi nn 4 fights brought yacht oils choice void beginning cannot connection
ht oi nn 5 His daughter had some insight in planning to buy penny oil stock.

ob rg un 6 objectives lobster problems large organize urge bounced tribunals
ob rg un 7 Often those who hunger for mobile action target mostly traveling.

ms au xp 8 forms himself terms author faulty haul expand taxpayer unexplored
ms au xp 9 Gems in museums are beautiful and augment the experiences of art.

25c LISTEN AND KEY

Directions Listen to the phrase, and then key it as a single unit. Key the space following a word as part of the word.
Option Key the phrases as they flash on your screen.

10 a pair | is ever | on hand | if only | to join | so vast | no fuel | is ever so
11 as you | as you | as you set | as you set up | as you set up the displays
12 as you set up | the displays for fall | be sure to focus | on the theme

25d SPEED SPRINTS

Directions Key from the software screen. You will have a limited time between attempts before the next timing begins. Keep focused.
Goal Strive to maintain your 15" speed on three 20" timings.

Key Point | Balanced-hand words help you to develop the muscle strength you need for maximum speed.

13 The county may dismantle the big signs if the work done is right.
balanced hand 14 They could make their goals if the workers bury their skepticism.
15 They may take the neighbor with a neuritis problem to the clinic.

45e 1' SPEED WRITING ↑↑

Directions

1. Take a 1' timing; key from the textbook. If you finish before time is up, begin again.
2. Repeat the timing 3 more times, trying to increase your rate. Key from the screen. A marker will indicate where you need to be at the end of each 15" in order to reach your goal. You will have 10" between attempts.

A

gwam 1'

If you have decided that a job change is right for you, exit	12
planning can be helpful. Here are some suggestions for you. Hold	26
off on announcing your exit until you have a solid offer from your	39
new employer. Two or three weeks' notice before leaving is common	52
courtesy. Prepare your letter with this time frame in mind, and	65
include the specific exit date. Keep the letter succinct and do	78
not take it personally if you are terminated immediately upon re-	91
ceipt of the letter. This may be company policy. Good luck to you.	104

1' | 1 | 2 | 3 | 4 | 5 | 6 | 7 | 8 | 9 | 10 | 11 | 12 | 13 |

45f SUSTAINED WRITING

Directions

1. Key a 2' writing, beginning with paragraph 1. Key from the textbook.
2. Key another 2' writing, beginning with paragraph 2. If you finish before time is up, start over with paragraph 1. Key from the textbook.
3. Key a 3' writing on the entire writing. Try to maintain your average 2' rate.

A

gwam 3'

Restaurants have a tendency to serve enormous portions of	4
food. People feel that to get the value of the money spent they	8
should consume it all. This may encourage some people to consume	13
too much food during any single serving. This has affected the	17
weight of people at every age level, even those in their teens.	21
Amazingly, one study indicated that at least one fifth of those in	26
that age group have a tendency to weigh more than they should. The	30
older generations are also showing a real overweight problem.	34
Without question, we just tend to consume too much food when	38
we are dining at a restaurant that serves large portions. As we	43
learn more about nutrition and the relationship of its content to	47
our good health, we must be willing to accept the facts and act for	52
that reason. Concerning the overweight problem, we can consider	56
sharing an entree with our dining partner. Don't be shy about re-	60
questing to share. If you like, consider tipping a little extra.	65
Eating less and watching content are important contributions to	69
controlling weight. Take care of your body; it is the only one you	74
will ever have.	75

3' | 1 | 2 | 3 | 4 |

25e 1' SPEED WRITING ↑ ↑

A

Directions

1. Take a 1' timing; key from the textbook. If you finish before time is up, begin again.
2. Repeat the timing 3 more times, trying to increase your rate. Key from the screen.

gwam   1'

Paris is known for its many small exquisite chocolate shops. 12
On our first day in the city, we made it a point to visit one of 25
the many nearby. I couldn't wait to request something mouthwater- 38
ing. I ordered their special, the Extraordinary, Double Hot Choco- 52
late. The waitress returned with a very large portion of dark 64
chocolate ice cream, with hot fudge smothering it, and a big red 77
cherry on top of it. She did not bring the dessert I had expected, 91
but the dessert she brought was really excellent. I would order it 104
again and again! 108

1' | 1 | 2 | 3 | 4 | 5 | 6 | 7 | 8 | 9 | 10 | 11 | 12 | 13 |

25f SUSTAINED WRITING

A

Directions

1. Key a 2' writing, beginning with paragraph 1. Key from the textbook.
2. Key another 2' writing, beginning with paragraph 2. If you finish before time is up, start over with paragraph 1. Key from the textbook.
3. Key a 3' writing on the entire writing. Try to maintain your average 2' rate.

gwam   3'

Advancing in your job requires that you identify some personal 4
goals. Without goals, any advancement may be difficult to achieve
and possibly be aimless. Ask yourself these questions: How can I
accelerate quickly in my present job and not cause a problem with 13
my associates? Who can give me the most assistance in my efforts? 18
How can I prepare myself? Will it require more experience or edu- 22
cation? How should I embark on my efforts for success in my cur- 26
rent job and gain the added skills that I need for a promotion? 31
35

To realize gains from any of the answers, you need to make a 39
concentrated effort to assess your situation realistically. You 43
must be emotionally ready to assume additional responsibility. 47
Know for sure that you want the position you are working to 51
achieve. Then focus extra attention on those answers that will 56
best help you improve your skills and abilities in what you are do- 60
ing. Be inclined to ask for help in areas where you need it. Most 65
of all, develop a compelling desire to be successful in all you do. 69

3' | 1 | 2 | 3 | 4 |

LESSON 45 | Speed Emphasis

45a Warmup

Directions Key each line twice from the textbook. Strive for accuracy the first time and try to improve your speed or fluency the second time.

alphabet 1 By winning off prizes Doug shows Kimm just exactly every quality.

fig/sym 2 Six precincts (13, 28, 149, and 165) received 72 ballots by 4:30.

speed 3 Neither Nathan nor Nelson knew the new announcer on that network.

> Key Point
> Digraphs are any two-letter combinations. Each combination requires a different physical movement. Practicing common digraphs helps you key two-letter combinations quickly.

45b TECHNIQUE BUILDER

Directions Key from the software screen. You will practice common letter pairs and then strive to increase your speed.
Goal Increase speed by 2 *gwam* and stay within the error limit.

dq tb sr 4 headquarter hindquarters outbid textbook misread disrupt newsreel

dq tb sr 5 The basketball headquarters was located near their new classroom.

lb nh sb 6 albums rollback bulbs unhappy downhill unheard asbestos passbooks

lb nh sb 7 Her husband sailed their sailboat with both its new enhancements.

yd km ez 8 honeydew everyday heyday milkman stockmen workman bezel squeezing

yd km ez 9 Payday for the workmen was not stopped because of the big freeze.

45c LISTEN AND KEY

Directions Listen to the phrase, and then key it as a single unit. Key the space following a word as part of the word.
Option Key the phrases as they flash on your screen.

10 they laugh | they laugh while others | they laugh while others fidget

11 both firms | audit them | they blame | field work | fish make | both profit

12 will workers reduce | and quickly recover | from this type of mistake

45d SPEED SPRINTS

Directions Key from the software screen. You will have a limited time between attempts before the next timing begins. Keep focused.
Goal Strive to maintain your 15" speed on three 20" timings.

13 Go on the autobus to the cozy spa with the dismal sorority girls.

balanced hand 14 Quantity may be the way to make soap but use handiwork for gowns.

15 The height of the man did make for a tight fit in the small auto.

Accuracy Emphasis

26a Warmup

Directions Key each line twice from the textbook. Strive for accuracy the first time and try to improve your speed or fluency the second time.

alphabet 1 Pat is dazzled by the jovial boxer who fights main bouts quickly.

fig/sym 2 Inventory Item #C-8329 (overhead) on page 406 is now in Room 157.

accuracy 3 It still seems illogical that their union action was so carefree.

26b TECHNIQUE BUILDER

Directions Key from the software screen. Additional practice lines will display if you do not meet your accuracy goal. Key accurately.

og ys lt 4 Jogging programs that guys do are built on fine physical results.

og ys lt 5 dog logic progress crystal always physics salts poultry multiples

iz oa dr 6 The size of the prize boat floats dreams of drifting on vacation.

iz oa dr 7 citizen finalize legalize oak roads toaster draw address druggist

af ok kn 8 After a committee acknowledged the new craft textbooks it was OK.

af ok kn 9 affair draft safely okay joke look knowledge doorknobs sicknesses

26c ACCURACY BUILDER

Directions Key from the software screen. You will have three attempts to key each sentence within the accuracy limits.

10 For better nutrition try to eat more fresh fruits and vegetables.

11 Ramon gave Tomas a hearty greeting at our neighbor's beach party.

12 Your friend, Beth Cummings, ought to study nursing in the future.

Press On

Keying is a mental function as well as a physical one. Controlling errors is a complex task. Generally the most frequent error is the simple misstroke, often caused by:

- Imperfect reach techniques
- Too much speed and faltering rhythm or anxiety
- Improper conditioners, such as posture, fingernails, and chair height

Visualize yourself keying calmly, quickly, and accurately. Say to yourself, "I enjoy keying and I am improving." See yourself as sitting erect, concentrating on what you are doing, and discovering new levels of skill.

"The control center of your life is your attitude."

Anonymous

44e 1' SPEED WRITING

Directions
1. Take a 1' timing; key from the textbook. If you finish before time is up, begin again.
2. Repeat the timing 3 more times, trying to increase your rate. Key from the screen.

A

gwam 1'

Paleontologists and archaeologists are not sure how many mil- 12
lions of years ago a human evolved, but have you ever thought about 26
how lucky you are to be alive? You really had your beginning not 39
only with your parents but also with the first human being. If you 52
consider the continuation of a lineage occurring every twenty years 66
during just one of those million years, each pairing had to be ex- 78
actly as it was approximately fifty thousand times. No matter the 91
circumstance, each pair of parents gave you life. Just as branches 105
of a tree die and end their journey of life, so did many of the 118
branches of human life. What an amazing miracle journey for each 131
living person today. 135

1' | 1 | 2 | 3 | 4 | 5 | 6 | 7 | 8 | 9 | 10 | 11 | 12 | 13 |

44f SUSTAINED WRITING

Directions
1. Key a 2' writing, beginning with paragraph 1. Key from the textbook.
2. Key another 2' writing, beginning with paragraph 2. Key from the textbook.
3. Key a 3' writing on the entire writing. Try to maintain your average 2' rate.

A

gwam 3'

Very few students pursue a keyboarding course today merely to 4
acquire a skill to get a job. Most students now realize that in 8
order to key computer data rapidly, they need to know how to use 13
the alphabetic keys using the touch system. It is important that a 17
person concentrate on the copy or the screen rather than on his or 22
her keyboard. While some people may excel more than others, the 26
minimum acquired speed should be faster than your handwriting speed 31
of approximately twenty-four words a minute. Only then will the 35
skill be a real advantage for your personal needs at home as well 39
as your business needs at work. 42

Hopefully if you are in a high school, you will have the op- 45
portunity to enroll in a keyboarding course in a computer labora- 50
tory. Often the course is simply a case of finding a time zone 54
within a student's course schedule. If you are not in a secondary 58
school environment, the school may have an excellent evening adult 63
education keyboarding course. Even students in the lower grades 67
can now profit from a quality early course in keyboarding, since 72
most students have access to computers both at home and at school. 76
Good skills at the keyboard learned at any time will really pay off 81
as you start applying your skills. 83

3' | 1 | 2 | 3 | 4 |

26d 1' ACCURACY WRITING ↑↑

A

Directions
1. Take a 1' timing; key from the textbook. If you finish before time is up, begin again.
2. Take three additional timings, keying from the software screen. Follow the directions in the software. The software will challenge you to either increase speed or accuracy.

gwam   1'

The drivers of chariots, buggies, and other early forms of | 12
transportation drivers did not have horns to sound. Horns came | 25
with the development of the automobile; they were used to scare the | 38
wits out of horses. As cars replaced horse transportation, people | 52
started using horns on unsuspecting citizens. They were used to | 65
tell people of a possible problem or to tell them to get out of | 77
their way; thus, the beginning of a new behavior called road rage. | 91
It can be started at any stop light when a toot is heard from be- | 104
hind as the red light is in the process of turning to green. This | 117
can trigger immediate rage and dangerous movements into the inter- | 130
section. Here is hoping you use your horn responsibly. | 141

1' | 1 | 2 | 3 | 4 | 5 | 6 | 7 | 8 | 9 | 10 | 11 | 12 | 13 |

26e SUSTAINED WRITING

A

Directions
1. Key a 2' writing, beginning with paragraph 1. Key from the textbook.
2. Key another 2' writing, beginning with paragraph 2. If you finish before time is up, start over with paragraph 1. Key from the textbook.
3. Key a 3' writing on the entire writing. If you finish before time is up, start over with paragraph 1.

Goal Try to maintain your average 2' *gwam* for 3'.

gwam   3'

Problem solving can be exciting and rewarding, regardless of | 4
how difficult the problem is. The critical aspect in solving a | 8
problem may not lie in the problem itself but in the person who | 13
faces the problem. You should have a winning attitude and be per- | 17
sistent to the end. When facing a problem, quietly stay in control | 21
as you analyze the situation and always believe that you can handle | 26
it. Keep the facts straight, remember to keep an open mind, and be | 31
willing to change your position if the factors warrant. | 34

You will discover that having a plan is important to coming to | 38
a satisfactory solution. You may find it useful to jot down and | 43
number the main elements of your problem as you identify them. Try | 47
to prioritize these elements as well as you can. This may facili- | 52
tate your outlining a solution later. Try to pinpoint especially | 56
the important parts that you have the power to change as you work | 60
through the challenging parts of the dilemma. Don't be impatient; | 65
it may take time for your plan to solve the problem. | 68

3' | 1 | 2 | 3 | 4 |

Speed Emphasis

Directions Key each line twice from the textbook. Strive for accuracy the first time and try to improve your speed or fluency the second time.

alphabet 1 The quick white dog is fearful of jumping over the grey box maze.

fig/sym 2 Invoice #25-376 (due 4/08) totaled $950 plus a hefty 10% penalty.

speed 3 I'll try to keep the sublet when they return; email me from home.

44b TECHNIQUE BUILDER

Directions Key from the software screen. You will practice common letter pairs and then strive to increase your speed.

Goal Increase speed by 2 *gwam* and stay within the error limit.

yw yc hb 4 entryway plywood haywire boycotts paychecks wishbone switchboards

yw yc hb 5 You can ride your new motorcycle everywhere in this neighborhood.

zo nx bv 6 zoo razor zone jinxing anxiety pharynx obviate obvious subversion

zo nx bv 7 Obviously as he flew westward he anxiously looked at the horizon.

yb yh ja 8 anybody soybean maybe keyhole greyhounds pajama jargon windjammer

yb yh ja 9 Maybe in my young boyhood years I would have worn a small jacket.

44c LISTEN AND KEY

Directions Listen to the phrase, and then key it as a single unit. Key the space following a word as part of the word.

Option Key the phrases as they flash on your screen.

 Key Point | Dictation is an external way of pacing your keying speed. The objective is to key phrases not letter by letter or word by word. Think phrases and watch your speed grow.

10 turn down | turn down the chance | follow my | follow my diet for a day

11 torn map | the torn map | they did sign | they both work | hand the sign |

12 I know why | I should follow my diet | and not eat | many of the snacks

44d SPEED SPRINTS

Directions Key from the software screen. You will have a limited time between attempts before the next timing begins. Keep focused.

Goal Strive to maintain your 15" speed on three 20" timings.

13 Select the right ritual flame to burn at the big coalfield sight.

balanced hand 14 Antique maps make handy visuals to hang for an endowment meeting.

15 The chairman will make a lamb out of the auditor when he reports.

LESSON 27

Accuracy Emphasis

27a Warmup

Directions Key each line twice from the textbook. Strive for accuracy the first time and try to improve your speed or fluency the second time.

alphabet 1 Two guards quickly arrived just when the man found my prized box.
fig/sym 2 Ty's shop had Item #9076 on sale for $8.15 (limit 2) through 3/4.
accuracy 3 Deciding to go deer hunting, Andrew excitedly dialed his friends.

27b TECHNIQUE BUILDER

Directions Key from the software screen. Additional practice lines will display if you do not meet your accuracy goal. Key accurately.

 Key Point | Your challenge is to attain speed on digraphs, the smallest keying elements possible. This is both a mental and physical challenge.

tm br dd 4 The postman brings your mail to your house if properly addressed.
tm br dd 5 investment postmark utmost break library hombre added fiddle odds

ks wn vo 6 Thanks for the rundown on those music favorites of the teenagers.
ks wn vo 7 locks checks looks own township known invoice devotes involvement

nl dy tw 8 Suddenly everybody in their twenties wanted to see his new movie.
nl dy tw 9 only openly humanly dye midyear study twelfth twilight eastwardly

27c ACCURACY BUILDER

Directions Key from the software screen. You will have three attempts to key each sentence within the accuracy limits.

10 Ike decided Cecilia did, indeed, like the five identical kittens.
11 Nine cadets did kid that kicker before the kickoff at Kyle Field.
12 The editors decided to edit an article identifying two hijackers.

43e 1' SPEED WRITING

↟
↟

Directions

1. Take a 1' timing; key from the textbook. If you finish before time is up, begin again.
2. Repeat the timing 3 more times, trying to increase your rate. Key from the screen.

gwam   1'

Recently, as I placed items in the trunk of my car, I acciden-   12
tally let one item fall to the ground. When I recovered the item,   26
I used the hand that held my keys. I placed both the keys and the   39
item in the trunk and closed it. This particular automobile auto-   52
matically locks all of the doors with this simple operation. When   65
help reached me, the rescue person said, "Oh no! Not that model."   79
I now have a perfect understanding of his reaction after several   92
long minutes listening to the emergency horn sounding on and off   105
repeatedly. A half-hour later he finally did get the door open,   118
but guess who called during the process? My wife! It was embar-   131
rassing to explain the situation with an emergency horn honking in   144
the background.   147

1' | 1 | 2 | 3 | 4 | 5 | 6 | 7 | 8 | 9 | 10 | 11 | 12 | 13 |

43f SUSTAINED WRITING

Directions

1. Key a 2' writing, beginning with paragraph 1. Key from the textbook.
2. Key another 2' writing, beginning with paragraph 2. Key from the textbook.
3. Key a 3' writing on the entire writing. Try to maintain your average 2' rate.

gwam   3'

Many employment applicants often realize after the fact that   4
they should have done more to prepare for an interview. Forming   8
some sharp answers in advance to a few typical interview questions   13
can help. For example, contemplate how you might respond to the   17
following questions: What do I know about the company and the em-   22
ployment I seek? Why am I interested in this position? How do   26
what I have been taught and my capabilities relate to the employ-   30
ment? What do I plan to be doing five years from now? What do I   34
do for relaxation and recreation? Do I plan any self-improvement   39
or company related courses in the future?   42

How is my work experience relevant to the position? What spe-   46
cific examples can I give? What unique personal traits and various   50
abilities do I have to bring to the organization? What are my ca-   55
reer objectives, and how are they relevant to both the firm and the   59
position I seek? What are some of my strong and weak capabilities?   64
It is important to bear in mind these questions are intended for   68
preparation. Do not tender answers to questions that are not asked   73
by interviewers. They are not interested in what you may think is   77
important. They are interested in their own questions.   81

3' | 1 | 2 | 3 | 4 |

27d 1' ACCURACY WRITING ↑ ↑

A

Directions

1. Take a 1' timing; key from the textbook. If you finish before time is up, begin again.
2. Take three additional timings, keying from the software screen. Follow the directions in the software. The software will challenge you to either increase speed or accuracy.

	gwam	1'

If you should employ a person in the future, pay attention to   12

the potential of the person to commit as a way to expect how well   26

the person will do in the position. Motivation is a vital part of   39

the interview and is often ignored. It is a most important part in   53

gauging how well the person will stand out in a company. As an em-   66

ployer, look for these characteristics: flexibility, a readiness   79

to take direction, an attraction for the work, emotional maturity,   92

a positive disposition, and confidence in the ability to succeed.   106

As an employer, you should always look for the traits that make   118

people more likely to be fully engaged in their work.   129

1' | 1 | 2 | 3 | 4 | 5 | 6 | 7 | 8 | 9 | 10 | 11 | 12 | 13 |

27e SUSTAINED WRITING

A

Directions

1. Key a 2' writing, beginning with paragraph 1. Key from the textbook.
2. Key another 2' writing, beginning with paragraph 2. If you finish before time is up, start over with paragraph 1. Key from the textbook.
3. Key a 3' writing on the entire writing. If you finish before time is up, start over with paragraph 1.

Goal Try to maintain your average 2' *gwam* for 3'.

	gwam	3'

Today, college freshman orientation may include much more than   4

just finding out the location of buildings or how to drop a course.   9

While the heart of the typical session may still deal with the ex-   13

citing new academic and social climate of college, it may also in-   17

clude an issue or two of real-world concern, such as topics on   22

health, safe conduct, and cultural diversity. The problem of time   26

management for those who might have to work or how to live with a   31

roommate may also be topics. Such topics may address normal but   35

possible problems of life at school.   37

Schools are eager to convey the quality of life they offer,   41

but they also want to avert problems that might make students not   46

want to continue. Some issues are much more complex than they were   50

just a few years ago, and student experience prior to going to col-   55

lege has seen drastic change. Officials who select mature topics   59

realize that students may need to hear some truths. One example is   64

the issue of plagiarism, the way it is dealt with, and its possible   68

consequences. This issue has intensified because of copying from   73

the Internet. Another, as the college population increases, is   77

that available housing may become a real problem.   80

3' | 1 | 2 | 3 | 4 |

LESSON 43   Speed Emphasis

43a   Warmup

Directions Key each line twice from the textbook. Strive for accuracy the first time and try to improve your speed or fluency the second time.

alphabet 1   Next to the grazing cow we passed a very unique farm Key Jubilee.

fig/sym 2   Pages 42, 153, 168, 279, and 304 are missing from that used book.

speed 3   We assumed he would rather hear about the chaos than the clutter.

43b   TECHNIQUE BUILDER

Directions Key from the software screen. You will practice common letter pairs and then strive to increase your speed.
Goal Increase speed by 2 *gwam* and stay within the error limit.

dw xh nw 4   dwelling midway speedway exhaust exhibit exhibits unwise downward

dw xh nw 5   Nationwide people's goodwill is exhibited by giving to charities.

sq kg ln 6   squat squid square backgammon backgrounds walnut kiln helpfulness

sq kg ln 7   A background of several severe illnesses may disqualify a person.

hd mf tn 8   birthday watchdog withdrew comfort discomfort witness correctness

hd mf tn 9   If she withdraws it can be very harmful to their new partnership.

43c   LISTEN AND KEY

Directions Listen to the phrase, and then key it as a single unit. Key the space following a word as part of the word.
Option Key the phrases as they flash on your screen.

10   does he have | does he have the | does he have the latest information

11   did she laugh | did she laugh while he | did she laugh while he spoke

12   I was sure Thomas saw | some pretty silk flowers | at the import shop

43d   SPEED SPRINTS

Directions Key from the software screen. You will have a limited time between attempts before the next timing begins. Keep focused.
Goal Strive to maintain your 15" speed on three 20" timings.

Key Point	The fastest and easiest words to type are balanced-hand words. Every other letter in the word is struck by a finger on the opposite hand.

13   Suspend the girl for the work she did not do on their proxy form.

balanced hand 14   She did envy the girls in the sorority and wants to sign with it.

15   The chairman did risk the chance the clemency amendment may fail.

LESSON 28

Accuracy Emphasis

28a Warmup

Directions Key each line twice from the textbook. Strive for accuracy the first time and try to improve your speed or fluency the second time.

alphabet 1 Five extra shallots were picked quickly for my big jaunt to Zion.

fig/sym 2 Box #5 measured 24″ × 36″ × 18″ and held 970 trays ($13.95 each).

accuracy 3 We started at a minimum wage based only upon stated average data.

 Key Point | Keep hands quiet; keep fingers curved and upright to attain your best speed.

28b TECHNIQUE BUILDER

Directions Key from the software screen. Additional practice lines will display if you do not meet your accuracy goal. Key accurately.

gn hr ze 4 Doug had long assignments throughout dozens of classes last year.

gn hr ze 5 gnarled dignity foreign shrimp throw shreds zero dozens formalize

xt ju gu 6 Some textiles in my judgment determine the style for good design.

xt ju gu 7 extras mixture context juices injuries unjust guard figure tongue

py ft gs 8 Send a draft copy of the findings to all departments for an okay.

py ft gs 9 pyramids lumpy poppy after fifths sift flagship pigskin standings

28c ACCURACY BUILDER

Directions Key from the software screen. You will have three attempts to key each sentence within the accuracy limits.

10 Quietly try to report to Peter two or three prior pottery errors.

11 All fall as a gag. Asa's dad sold old, odd glass flasks as gifts.

12 Did a mob nab a zany miner and his box of zinc or mica in a cave?

42e 1' SPEED WRITING ↑ ↑

A

Directions

1. Take a 1' timing; key from the textbook. If you finish before time is up, begin again.
2. Repeat the timing 3 more times, trying to increase your rate. Key from the screen.

gwam 1'

At lunch there were two women at the next table having a con-	12
versation in a foreign language. I couldn't understand one single	25
word but each voice was pleasant sounding. It was like listening	39
to music; just like birds singing. I can't understand a word of	51
their music either. Do birds have a language? I needed to know.	65
Back at the office I went to the Internet, the holder of all infor-	78
mation. Can you believe there were several pages of links to web-	91
sites about bird language? Generally speaking, there are five	104
categories of bird language. I have been giving much thought to	117
the subject and I still don't understand how researchers know what	130
birds are thinking.	134

1' | 1 | 2 | 3 | 4 | 5 | 6 | 7 | 8 | 9 | 10 | 11 | 12 | 13 |

42f SUSTAINED WRITING

A

Directions

1. Key a 2' writing, beginning with paragraph 1. Key from the textbook.
2. Key another 2' writing, beginning with paragraph 2.
3. Key a 3' writing on the entire writing. Try to maintain your average 2' rate.

gwam 3'

In an effort to improve their quality of life, young and old	4
alike continue to show great interest in some kind of physical ac-	8
tivity during their leisure time. Many forms of exercise may range	13
from walking at a fast stride to taking part in a jazzercise class.	17
A new diet often is part of any change in health habits also, since	22
a change in lifestyle usually is called for. The lifestyle change	26
is probably the most difficult part to accomplish. It is easy to	31
start the change, but sustaining it over time is most challenging.	35
A holiday, vacation, or some other alteration in your customary	40
routine can turn one back to an old habit. Be persistent.	44
Changes in an individual's physical condition should be made	48
slowly. It is tempting to try too hard to change one's physical	52
status too quickly, which can cause more harm than good. Anyone	56
who may desire to make a drastic or sudden change in lifestyle	60
needs to consult with a qualified expert or doctor first for full	65
approval. Obviously the main rule is to proceed slowly so that	69
your body can adjust. Monitor your activity; keep daily records,	74
zoning in on the amount of time you spend on your physical activ-	78
ity. Also monitor such things as your weight, heartbeat, and	82
blood pressure. Above all, vary the activity to make it enjoyable.	87

3' | 1 | 2 | 3 | 4 |

28d 1' ACCURACY WRITING ↑ ↑

A

Directions
1. Take a 1' timing; key from the textbook. If you finish before time is up, begin again.
2. Take three additional timings, keying from the software screen. Follow the directions in the software. The software will challenge you to either increase speed or accuracy.

gwam 1'

It is possible to have a ten minute conversation with an an-   12
swering machine directing caller traffic and never have a discus-   25
sion with a real person. You know what I mean: "If you are call-   38
ing about healthcare information, press one." You can press num-   50
bers forever and seemingly never contact the person who can help   63
you. Yes, understandably, the machines save a lot of labor costs.   77
But I wonder how much business a company may lose because people   90
became disgusted and hung up, or the caller forgot the reason they 103
called in the first place. Oh, for the good old days when real   116
people answered the phone and you didn't have to use your finger to 130
do the talking.   133

1' | 1 | 2 | 3 | 4 | 5 | 6 | 7 | 8 | 9 | 10 | 11 | 12 | 13 |

28e SUSTAINED WRITING

A

Directions
1. Key a 2' writing, beginning with paragraph 1. Key from the textbook.
2. Key another 2' writing, beginning with paragraph 2. If you finish before time is up, start over with paragraph 1. Key from the textbook.
3. Key a 3' writing on the entire writing. If you finish before time is up, start over with paragraph 1.
Goal Try to maintain your average 2' *gwam* for 3'.

gwam 3'

Perhaps you have heard the term "empowerment" and wondered   4
what the word means. Empowerment is one of those "buzz" words used   8
to explain not a program but a system that draws upon the values   13
and beliefs of all involved. Empowerment occurs when every person   17
in the organization feels as if he or she plays an important role   22
in the organization's overall success. Workers who believe their   26
work is important will strive to do their best. Empowerment also   30
gives each person a sense of confidence or self-esteem; a great re- 35
turn for each person.   36

An empowered group seeks to place decision making at the most   40
practical level and gives solid support to the decisions made at   45
that level. To make just decisions, each person in the organiza-   49
tion must clearly understand the group's true mission and goals;   53
and every member must have a clear picture of the unique part he or 58
she will play to help realize those goals. The synergy created is   62
remarkable. Synergy in this situation means the working together   67
of two or more people to bring about a result greater than the sum 71
of their individual effects or capabilities.   74

3' | 1 | 2 | 3 | 4 |

LESSON 42

Speed Emphasis

42a Warmup

Directions Key each line twice from the textbook. Strive for accuracy the first time and try to improve your speed or fluency the second time.

alphabet	1	Copying examples just before we give a quiz makes students happy.
fig/sym	2	New locker keys for #30, #56, #147, and #289 were ordered Monday.
speed	3	One viable option was to delay his desire to retire to your city.

> **Key Point** Your challenge is to attain speed on digraphs, the smallest keying elements possible. This is both a mental and physical challenge.

42b TECHNIQUE BUILDER

Directions Key from the software screen. You will practice common letter pairs and then strive to increase your speed.
Goal Increase speed by 2 *gwam* and stay within the error limit.

gy wt np	4	gym energy strategy newt regrowth pewter unpaid tinplates unpack.
gy wt np	5	The unparalleled growth in the application of psychology is good.
fs ah gm	6	cliffs offsets proofs mahogany ahead segments judgments augmented
fs ah gm	7	Karah holds beliefs and acknowledgments ahead of other interests.
mn yr vy	8	columns condemnation hymns pyres payrolls styrene navy heavy levy
mn yr vy	9	A large gymnastics playroom was the envy of all the neighborhood.

42c LISTEN AND KEY

Directions Listen to the phrase, and then key it as a single unit. Key the space following a word as part of the word.
Option Key the phrases as they flash on your screen.

10	the right mix | the right mix of | speed and accuracy | reach your goal
11	blend the right mix | of speed and accuracy | to reach your new goals
12	it is fun | to be on a winning team | winning takes effort | every time

42d SPEED SPRINTS

Directions Key from the software screen. You will have a limited time between attempts before the next timing begins. Keep focused.
Goal Strive to maintain your 15" speed on three 20" timings.

	13	The eight girl pals did form the work panel for the downtown dig.
balanced hand	14	She will pay half the cost of the ham for the formal city social.
	15	Glen did buy an antique lens to make wide angle visuals of autos.

LESSON 29

Accuracy Emphasis

29a Warmup

Directions Key each line twice from the textbook. Strive for accuracy the first time and try to improve your speed or fluency the second time.

alphabet 1 K. C. Quip was vexed when I found my lazy cat on his blue Jaguar.
fig/sym 2 The savings on Items #19, #27, #36, and #48 (at 50%) will be $90.
accuracy 3 The rest can verify my interest in where the sign may be erected.

29b TECHNIQUE BUILDER

Directions Key from the software screen. Additional practice lines will display if you do not meet your accuracy goal. Key accurately.

oy cy ph 4 The efficiency of that photographer was a joy to watch yesterday.
oy cy ph 5 royal boys employ cycle fancy secrecy pharmacy pamphlet monograph

wr rl my 6 Don't overlook using your old typewriter to key my new envelopes.
wr rl my 7 Wrong showroom unwrap world darling girl mysteries myself economy

jo lp sk 8 His journey to the Alps for alpine skiing turned out to be great.
jo lp sk 9 joker major enjoy alpha helpfully gulp skeptical basketball risks

29c ACCURACY BUILDER

Directions Key from the software screen. You will have three attempts to key each sentence within the accuracy limits.

 Key Point | This drill consists of many words involving the second and third fingers. The purpose is to develop quickly the memory pattern between keys that involve those fingers.

10 Opal plans to assist Lowell as he waxes his jazzy, aqua sailboat.
11 Last fall I saw Sally dash away your plans to fix the pool table.
12 Two opposed all loan opportunities zealously; a tax is the issue.

41e 1' SPEED WRITING

↑
↑

Directions

1. Take a 1' timing; key from the textbook. If you finish before time is up, begin again.
2. Repeat the timing 3 more times, trying to increase your rate. Key from the screen.

A

	gwam	1'
A successful and fulfilling life has several dimensions to it.		13
In general, the notable ones are length, depth, and breadth. Your		26
length of life may depend upon how you take care of the genes you		39
received at birth. Depth is finding success in your work or at		52
your job. Breadth is all of the experiences beyond your health and		66
survival to make your life pleasurable. Complete the dimensions in		79
your life and you will likely experience the feelings of very real		93
success and fulfillment.		98

1' | 1 | 2 | 3 | 4 | 5 | 6 | 7 | 8 | 9 | 10 | 41 | 12 | 13 |

41f SUSTAINED WRITING

Directions

1. Key a 2' writing, beginning with paragraph 1. Key from the textbook.
2. Key another 2' writing, beginning with paragraph 2. Key from the textbook.
3. Key a 3' writing on the entire writing. Try to maintain your average 2' rate.

A

	gwam	3'
Upon going into the x-ray section of a hospital, I was told		4
unconditionally by a very authoritative nurse to completely remove		8
all of my clothing except my shoes, put on a hospital gown, and		13
then go to the waiting room and wait approximately ten minutes.		17
The one size fits all garment was split from top to bottom, with		21
just two sets of fasteners. I decided quickly the split would be		26
in the back. I would tie the top set of fasteners and my hand		30
would make up for the second set that I could not fasten com-		34
pletely. Carefully protecting my dignity, I immediately made the		38
trip to the waiting room.		40
There were three men in the waiting room. Seeing the diffi-		44
cult circumstances, I joined two of them in an important weather		48
conversation. As we stood there using one hand to hold the back of		53
our gowns, we each visually acknowledged the gentleman with his		57
back against the wall reading. I thought he couldn't tie the fas-		62
teners. The nurse entered the room, and called out his name. He		66
did not grab the back of his gown, but he casually walked past us.		71
In perfect harmony we said "Oh!" He was wearing two gowns; one		75
front, one back. The weather conversation immediately continued.		79

3' | 1 | 2 | 3 | 4 |

LESSON 41 SPEED EMPHASIS

PART 1   79

29d 1' ACCURACY WRITING

Directions

1. Take a 1' timing; key from the textbook. If you finish before time is up, begin again.
2. Take three additional timings, keying from the software screen. Follow the directions in the software. The software will challenge you to either increase speed or accuracy.

	gwam	1'
Orchids are beautiful flowers, particularly the large cat-		11
tleya. For them to bloom in your home there has to be an appropri-		25
ate environment. They must have a suitable amount of light. Con-		38
stant air movement and a humidity balance are a necessity. For		50
about a month each year the temperature has to be just about fifty-		64
five degrees. They have to have a supply of water each week at the		77
right temperature. Also, they need something to cling to for them		91
to absorb their water and food from the air. I guess we are some-		104
what like the cattleya; we need our own unique environment for the		117
maximum bloom of our life.		122

1' | 1 | 2 | 3 | 4 | 5 | 6 | 7 | 8 | 9 | 10 | 11 | 12 | 13 |

29e SUSTAINED WRITING

Directions

1. Key a 2' writing, beginning with paragraph 1. Key from the textbook.
2. Key another 2' writing, beginning with paragraph 2. If you finish before time is up, start over with paragraph 1. Key from the textbook.
3. Key a 3' writing on the entire writing. If you finish before time is up, start over with paragraph 1.

Goal Try to maintain your average 2' gwam for 3'.

	gwam	3'
In the past few years, office workers have learned of the need		4
to pay closer attention to what they eat and how active and fit		8
they are. Fitness centers have sprung up all over the country.		13
Such places have special equipment and aerobic classes that are		17
meant to meet the fitness needs of most people, including those who		22
work during the day. A quality center offers workers a flexible		26
schedule of weight-training, water aerobic classes, and swimming.		30
Swimming has also become very popular just for the pleasure it of-		35
fers people of all ages.		36
Many firms realize how important it is for the health of work-		40
ers with desk jobs to get more physical exercise. They also real-		45
ize that the lack of mobility required of desk work may be one of		49
the contributors to the overweight problem of many workers. Today		54
it is not too unusual for some large firms to build exercise fa-		58
cilities on their premises for the employees. The facilities have		62
space and equipment available for workers before and after work.		67
Other firms may simply opt to urge their workers to join local fit-		71
ness centers that offer the firms a group rate.		74

3' | 1 | 2 | 3 | 4 |

LESSON 41

Speed Emphasis

41a Warmup

Directions Key each line twice from the textbook. Strive for accuracy the first time and try to improve your speed or fluency the second time.

alphabet 1 Sammy and Jan Quinn fixed up a big cozy room with a view to like.
fig/sym 2 Invoice #34-716 (due 9/12) totaled $800 plus a hefty 15% penalty.
speed 3 She cannot afford to amend the order and send for a new recorder.

41b TECHNIQUE BUILDER

Directions Key from the software screen. You will practice common letter pairs and then strive to increase your speed.
Goal Increase speed by 2 *gwam* and stay within the error limit.

41c LISTEN AND KEY

Directions Listen to the phrase, and then key it as a single unit. Key the space following a word as part of the word.
Option Key the phrases as they flash on your screen.

10 if the case | if the pool | if it was | if the rest is | if the facts are
11 with my work | with you both | with interest in | with concern for them
12 I used | my special checking account | to pay the charge | for my phone

41d SPEED SPRINTS

Directions Key from the software screen. You will have a limited time between attempts before the next timing begins. Keep focused.
Goal Strive to maintain your 15" speed on three 20" timings.

Timely Topic

Working Relationships

When you are starting a new job it is difficult to remember the many names of the people with whom you will be working. One way to remember names is to draw a diagram of the new space where you will be working. As you meet people, write down their name in the space on your diagram where they work. As you talk to a person and learn more about them (such as a child's name, etc.), write it down in his or her space on your diagram. You will develop a great working relationship quickly by knowing all the names.

© GETTY IMAGES/PHOTODISC

Assessment

30a Warmup

Directions Key each line twice from the textbook. Strive for accuracy the first time and try to improve your speed or fluency the second time.

alphabet 1 Win analyzed and proven tax benefits that justify my quick gains.
speed 2 It is questionable whether the reported possibilities are viable.
accuracy 3 That edition ran an editorial questioning the reporter's actions.

30b ACCURACY BUILDER

Directions Key these sentences from the software screen. You will have three attempts to key each sentence within the accuracy limits.

4 My brother, Johnny, ran many races before he graduated from Rice.
5 I concede my Uncle Bret must have lost my recent unlisted number.
6 Cecile brought many bright mums and ribbons to Bryan's gymnasium.

30c TIMED WRITING

Directions Key two 3' timings from the textbook. Review your errors if you made any. Complete the error diagnostic drills.

A

	gwam	3'	5'

You can use a number of approaches to attain job security once you are well along in your career with an organization. One of the best strategies is to develop contacts inside and outside your company. In a positive way, make sure your distinctive talents are known in the company and use them to your advantage. Also, perform some critical tasks that are exceptional, making you the expert and too valuable for replacement. Let it be known that you are a company person and want to be a part of the group.

Another approach is learning to communicate effectively. Anything you can do to help you to become a better speaker and writer will be worth the effort. Take an active part in clubs as an officer while in school to acquire some valuable experience, and seize every opportunity to continue to improve once you are employed. Be active in your community such as your local Chamber of Commerce or Red Cross. You can gain considerable influence in both your company and your community.

gwam	3'	5'
4	3	42
9	5	45
13	8	48
17	10	50
22	13	53
27	16	56
31	19	58
34	20	60
38	23	63
43	26	65
47	28	68
51	31	71
56	34	73
60	36	76
65	39	79
66	40	80

```
3' |    1    |    2    |    3    |    4    |
5' |      1      |      2      |      3      |
```

30d PACED WRITING

Directions Key the Paced Writing from the software. The software will begin at whatever level is appropriate for you. Try to reach your speed or accuracy goals.

Assessment

40a Warmup

Directions Key each line twice from the textbook. Strive for accuracy the first time and try to improve your speed or fluency the second time.

alphabet 1 Vicente disqualified zealous bikers who excitedly jumped the gun.

speed 2 In order to fulfill your requests, we hope that you will call us.

accuracy 3 Some of the others know of your interest in being part of a team.

40b ACCURACY BUILDER

Directions Key from the software screen. You will have three attempts to key each sentence within the accuracy limits.

40c TIMED WRITING

Directions Key two 3' timings from the textbook. Review your errors if you made any. Complete the error diagnostic drills.

		gwam	3'	5'

People who have a positive self-image usually have various `4 | 2 | 51`
things going for them. They have a realistic view about how much `8 | 5 | 54`
control they exert over events in everyday life. They are quite `13 | 8 | 56`
able to keep their emotions under control and adjust in stride to `17 | 10 | 59`
setbacks in life. They have a tolerant view toward themselves and `22 | 13 | 62`
others as well as high self-respect and self-confidence. They are `26 | 16 | 64`
able to deal with most situations that come along. In time, they `30 | 18 | 67`
will even enhance the situation in which they find themselves. `35 | 21 | 70`
People must realize that what we may consider a tragedy may be a `39 | 23 | 72`
blessing in disguise. A positive self-image is one of a person's `43 | 26 | 75`
most valuable assets. `45 | 27 | 76`

People who feel positive about their life are able to appreci- `49 | 29 | 78`
ate the positive and moral character found in others. Those who do `53 | 32 | 81`
not have a positive feeling and are dishonest emit a negative image `58 | 35 | 84`
and lose in the long run. These same qualities are in evidence in `62 | 37 | 86`
the dealings we have in business. In a business deal if a positive `67 | 40 | 89`
feeling of self-worth and honesty is not felt by both parties the `71 | 43 | 92`
deal will probably not be completed. Just remember trust makes `76 | 45 | 94`
business and our society work. It all starts with a positive feel- `80 | 48 | 97`
ing about one's self. `81 | 49 | 98`

| 3' | 1 | 2 | 3 | 4 |
| 5' | 1 | 2 | 3 |

40d PACED WRITING

Directions Key the Paced Writing from the software. The software will begin at whatever level is appropriate for you. Try to reach your speed or accuracy goals.

LESSON 31

Speed Emphasis

31a Warmup

Directions Key each line twice from the textbook. Strive for accuracy the first time and try to improve your speed or fluency the second time.

alphabet 1   Rex quickly emphasized the goals of various new jobs just posted.

fig/sym 2   Plumbing fixtures #4-62 and #8-90 go on sale on 3/17 reduced 50%.

speed 3   The city official has taken a firm stance since much is at stake.

31b TECHNIQUE BUILDER

Directions Key from the software screen. You will practice common letter pairs and then strive to increase your speed.

Goal Increase speed by 2 *gwam* and stay within the error limit.

31c LISTEN AND KEY

Directions Listen to the phrase, and then key it as a single unit. Key the space following a word as part of the word.

Option Key the phrases as they flash on your screen.

10   is up | up to | is up to | he was | was to | she was to | if you | you did well

11   so many men | do my job | come and go | so they are | to buy it | the world

12   please let me know | as soon as possible | when she will be available

31d SPEED SPRINTS

Directions Key from the software screen. You will have a limited time between attempts before the next timing begins. Keep focused.

Goal Strive to maintain your 15" speed on three 20" timings.

Timely Topic

© DIGITAL VISION

Ethics in the Workplace

Every day working professionals must make difficult ethical decisions on the job. Ethical decisions refer to an individual's ability to "do the right thing." Business ethics is a method of applying moral guidelines in the workplace. To encourage ethical behavior, companies develop a written code of ethics that outlines standards and consequences. A code of conduct focuses on relations with customers, employees, shareholders, suppliers, and the community. Companies frequently offer training to help employees make good ethical decisions.

39d 1' ACCURACY WRITING

Directions
1. Take a 1' timing; key from the textbook. If you finish before time is up, begin again.
2. Take three additional timings, keying from the software screen.

gwam   1'

On an adventure to Nantucket we took to the air from the   11
mainland in a ten passenger airplane. It was so small there was no   25
flight attendant. Instead, the cockpit was open so the pilots   38
could substitute. It was not a good procedure. It was so rough   51
the pilot was doing everything he could to stay in control The co-   64
pilot was concentrating on his materials, which had either instruc-   77
tion for how to keep us in the air or to discover where we were go-   90
ing. Halfway to our destination several people spilled their   103
drinks. The airplane was so unstable no one could give assistance.   116

1' | 1 | 2 | 3 | 4 | 5 | 6 | 7 | 8 | 9 | 10 | 11 | 12 | 13 |

39e SUSTAINED WRITING

Directions
1. Key a 2' writing, beginning with paragraph 1. Key from the textbook.
2. Key another 2' writing, beginning with paragraph 2. Key from the textbook.
3. Key a 3' writing on the entire writing. If you finish before time is up, start over with paragraph 1.

gwam   3'

Have you ever contemplated looking for a job in another coun-   4
try? If you have, you should realize that extra language lessons   8
just won't be enough. If you are to adjust moderately quickly to   13
life in a foreign country there is much more. Ideally you should   17
also acquaint yourself with the country's unique history, along   21
with the culture, traditions, and values of its people. Your work   26
life should be easier as you learn about the work habits and styles   30
of your new colleagues. Just remember to intermingle with the   35
population, as in the old saying, "While in Rome do as the Romans   39
do." You are not there to change their culture.   42

As the populations of our own cities, both large and small,   46
have become more diverse, we have improved in our sensitivity to   51
cultural differences. Certainly the more a person seeks out op-   55
portunities to work and to play with those of another race or cul-   59
ture, the more likely it is for that person to adjust smoothly in   64
any kind of job that requires moving to a foreign country. There   68
is no substitute for good communication. Before you leave, seek   72
people from the country you are going to and talk to them exten-   77
sively about what you may expect in the new country.   80

3' | 1 | 2 | 3 | 4 |

31e 1' SPEED WRITING

Directions
1. Take a 1' timing; key from the textbook. If you finish before time is up, begin again.
2. Repeat the timing 3 more times, trying to increase your rate. Key from the screen.

A

	gwam	1'

At some point in your life, your work may call upon you to   12
give a presentation. You must develop your own unique speaking   25
style. Generally you should divide your time between writing and   38
rehearsing aloud. Make sure that your opening and closing remarks   51
are entertaining. That will help you connect with your audience.   65
Practice your talk no fewer than five times. Practice until you   78
have the enunciation of your words correctly, and your voice sounds   91
like you believe what you are saying. Your non-verbal body lan-   104
guage should also be in step with what you are saying. Arrive at   117
the location of the presentation several minutes early. Check on   130
the lectern, the lighting, the sound, and any other equipment you   143
may be using; do not depend on someone else to do the checking.   156
When the time comes, break a leg.   163

1' | 1 | 2 | 3 | 4 | 5 | 6 | 7 | 8 | 9 | 10 | 11 | 12 | 13 |

31f SUSTAINED WRITING

Directions
1. Key a 2' writing, beginning with paragraph 1. Key from the textbook.
2. Key another 2' writing, beginning with paragraph 2. Key from the textbook.
3. Key a 3' writing on the entire writing. Try to maintain your average 2' rate.

A

	gwam	3'

If, in the course of your job search, you are offered two com-   4
parable jobs, how do you decide which job to take? You should   8
think over several factors as you compare the advantages and disad-   13
vantages of the jobs. The distance you will travel to and from   17
each job is one factor to consider. What are the working condi-   21
tions under which you may have to work in either job? You should   26
also compare the advancement opportunities between the two jobs.   30
Company size may be important to you. Salary is a leading factor   34
in the decision.   35

Before deciding which job to choose, also consider other as-   39
pects. These include the fringe benefits each job is offering.   44
Parking costs can be expensive if the firm does not have ample   48
parking for its workers. Is there a stock sharing option avail-   52
able? Be sure to inquire about what type of medical insurance the   57
company uses. How much does the company pay toward the cost of   61
medical insurance? Does the company help pay for your tuition if   65
you decide to go back to school or to attend a seminar?   68

3' | 1 | 2 | 3 | 4 |

LESSON 39   Accuracy Emphasis

39a   Warmup

Directions Key each line twice from the textbook. Strive for accuracy the first time and try to improve your speed or fluency the second time.

alphabet	1	Zane expects to pass five bylaws quickly during the June meeting.
fig/sym	2	Model Z-23-98 measures 15″ × 30″ × 46″ and costs $187 discounted.
accuracy	3	Much pomp will herald the performance of the engaged opera stars.

39b   TECHNIQUE BUILDER

Directions Key from the software screen. Additional practice lines will display if you do not meet your accuracy goal. Key accurately.

bb lc tg	4	An outgoing person who welcomes all hobbies has many new friends.
bb lc tg	5	lobby rabbits pebble ulcer balcony mulch mortgage outgo mortgages
az aj hn	6	He is amazed at the amount of math required of technology majors.
az aj hn	7	azaleas glazing lazy majestic pajamas majority doughnut technical
tf yl pf	8	Thoughtful styling is helpful in the placing of office furniture.
tf yl pf	9	catfish outfit artful nylon bylaw vinyl campfire leapfrogs capful

 Key Point | Do not practice using a metronomic stroking pattern. Let your own rhythm pattern emerge.

39c   ACCURACY BUILDER

Directions Key from the software screen. You will have three attempts to key each sentence within the accuracy limits.

10	Those youth in that sleek yacht surged ahead in the rough waters.
11	After many lessons nightly, the two got the routine down exactly.
12	I heard distinctly that the city will raze those unsightly ruins.

Speed Emphasis

32a Warmup

Directions Key each line twice from the textbook. Strive for accuracy the first time and try to improve your speed or fluency the second time.

alphabet 1 Maple gave Jack a quartz watch and an onyx ring for his birthday.

fig/sym 2 That * notes three missing checks (936, 1028, and 1457) on 12/10.

speed 3 Thank you very much for a copy of your letter to update my files.

32b TECHNIQUE BUILDER

Directions Key from the software screen. You will practice common letter pairs and then strive to increase your speed.
Goal Increase speed by 2 *gwam* and stay within the error limit.

sm xc bs 4 smiles cosmos criticism except excuses excels absent lambs scrubs

sm xc bs 5 Observe the excellent enthusiasm of the children cheering him on.

ps ek gl 6 psychiatry snapshot ups eking weekly seek glad mangle igloos ugly

ps ek gl 7 I had a glorious weekend with no mishaps; nothing but fun skiing.

je gg dy 8 jet project jewel eggnog suggests buggy dyeing handyman everybody

je gg dy 9 The lady wears jeans and puts her good clothes in baggage to fly.

32c LISTEN AND KEY

Directions Listen to the phrase, and then key it as a single unit. Key the space following a word as part of the word.
Option Key the phrases as they flash on your screen.

10 see him | if you | the pumps | did join | upon the | as she | my bid | pump gas

11 do my work | stop and go | if they are | to buy it | go by him | if so many

12 we knew last week | that you were | the top student | in the swim class

32d SPEED SPRINTS

Directions Key from the software screen. You will have a limited time between attempts before the next timing begins. Keep focused.
Goal Strive to maintain your 15" speed on three 20" timings.

| Key Point | Balanced-hand words help you to develop the muscle strength you need for maximum speed. |

13 If they wish she may do an audit for the firm in the big cubicle.

balanced hand 14 The chairman wished to pay for the usual bushels of corn and hay.

15 The lamb had a fight with the cow and eight doe in the cornfield.

38d 1' ACCURACY WRITING ↑↑

Directions
1. Take a 1' timing; key from the textbook. If you finish before time is up, begin again.
2. Take three additional timings, keying from the software screen.

gwam 1'

A home office can revitalize your life and career, offering 12
flexibility and more time with your family. But that won't amount 25
to much if the environment isn't advantageous to your work and fam- 38
ily. You need work space that is yours alone, not just a room that 52
doubles as an office and guest room or a tiny desk wedged into your 66
family room. Your work may require you to have a reliable Internet 79
connection rather than dial-up. Above all, your family must re- 92
spect your privacy when you are in your office. 101

1' | 1 | 2 | 3 | 4 | 5 | 6 | 7 | 8 | 9 | 10 | 11 | 12 | 13 |

38e SUSTAINED WRITING

Directions
1. Key a 2' writing, beginning with paragraph 1. Key from the textbook.
2. Key another 2' writing, beginning with paragraph 2. Key from the textbook.
3. Key a 3' writing on the entire writing. If you finish before time is up, start over with paragraph 1.

gwam 3'

At some point in your life you may be prompted to compose a 4
letter of complaint. To get the best results, consider how you 8
should begin your letter. Don't start by threatening legal action 13
or by stating what you will do if your complaint is not rectified. 17
If you truly feel that you are justified in seeking action and the 22
person handling your complaint will concur, the best opening remark 26
would be one in which you make your request. Any specific facts to 31
clarify your current situation should be pointed out next. 35

However, if you realize you must convince the recipient of 39
your letter that some kind of remedy is legitimate, a better opener 43
would be one that gets in step with your reader first. Find some- 47
thing good to say about the person receiving the letter; do not be 52
aggressively confrontational at this point. Check again the accuracy of 56
all of your facts carefully before composing the letter. 61
Write your letter when the evidence fully backs up your complaint. 65
The evidence should then be given in a firm but positive way. Fi- 69
nally, ask for action. Choose words carefully that will ensure 74
reader respect throughout your letter. 76

3' | 1 | 2 | 3 | 4 |

32e 1' SPEED WRITING

A

Directions
1. Take a 1' timing; key from the textbook. If you finish before time is up, begin again.
2. Repeat the timing 3 more times, trying to increase your rate. Key from the screen.

gwam   1'

Do you get to work feeling vigorous and by mid afternoon you	12
are tired and less productive? You aren't alone; many people have	26
a similar problem of feeling exhausted as the day wears on. There	39
are several things you can do to be more productive in late after-	52
noon. For instance, try to get fresh air sometime during the day.	66
Eat lunch outside or take a short walk. Don't skip a meal; this is	79
a sure way to diminish your energy quickly. Plan your work; com-	92
plete difficult responsibilities first; don't put them off until	105
later in the day. Conclusively, take a mental break periodically;	118
think about something else for a few minutes. It will rejuvenate	132
your mind.	134

1' | 1 | 2 | 3 | 4 | 5 | 6 | 7 | 8 | 9 | 10 | 11 | 12 | 13 |

32f SUSTAINED WRITING

A

Directions
1. Key a 2' writing, beginning with paragraph 1. Key from the textbook.
2. Key another 2' writing, beginning with paragraph 2. Key from the textbook.
3. Key a 3' writing on the entire writing. Try to maintain your average 2' rate.

gwam   3'

In today's business facts and figures are usually processed by	4
computers, but the people of a company are the ones who drive the	9
systems that keep a company running smoothly. Know what to expect	13
of the system and how to work with the information for maximum re-	17
sults. Think of yourself as playing a unique position on your	22
firm's team. Play this position to the utmost of your abilities.	26
If you are in charge of the firm's records, be absolutely sure	30
those records are exact. If assigned a report, do your very best	35
writing and concentrate on the probable use of the information.	39
As a team member, undoubtedly you will be held accountable for	43
completing all tasks assigned to you. When you are given an as-	47
signment, organize your work habits so that your job is completed	52
on time. Write down a schedule of when you think each phase of the	56
assignment should be completed. If needed, revise the schedule as	61
you work, then you will be ready should you be asked to do the as-	65
signment again in the future. Resist the desire to put off until	69
tomorrow what should be completed today. Do the most outstanding	74
work you are capable of doing so you can take pride in your final	78
product. This will make you an invaluable team member.	82

3' | 1 | 2 | 3 | 4 |

LESSON 38

Accuracy Emphasis

Directions Key each line twice from the textbook. Strive for accuracy the first time and try to improve your speed or fluency the second time.

alphabet 1 That crowd was quick to applaud five zany, ambidextrous jugglers.

fig/sym 2 Our Policy #280-5734 (amended) calls for annual payments of $196.

accuracy 3 I'm elated he has been selected to address those most interested.

38b TECHNIQUE BUILDER

Directions Key from the software screen. Additional practice lines will display if you do not meet your accuracy goal. Key accurately.

bm eb zi 4 Amazingly the celebration of the launch of the submarine was fun.

bm eb zi 5 cabman submarine resubmit ebony debit web zipper grazing magazine

rh yt hw 6 Perhaps daytime highway travel is the safest time to travel home.

rh yt hw 7 rhodium overhauls anything catalytic highways northwest forthwith

ka lw dj 8 Railways have a remarkable adjustment to make to stay profitable.

ka lw dj 9 okay alkali eureka always hallway millwork adject adjoin readjust

38c ACCURACY BUILDER

Directions Key from the software screen. You will have three attempts to key each sentence within the accuracy limits.

10 Our two groups were to take your tour, too; yet we were too late.

11 As Asa sadly said, Dallas hassled a jaded lad last fall as a gag.

12 Can Velez and Ruiz excavate their bauxite cavern in minimum time?

LESSON 33
Speed Emphasis

33a Warmup

Directions Key each line twice from the textbook. Strive for accuracy the first time and try to improve your speed or fluency the second time.

alphabet 1 Kim Bujnoch excitedly requested she verify each big prize winner.

fig/sym 2 My invoice #43-98 (12 caps at $5.89 each) totals $70.68 plus tax.

speed 3 What a thrill when the youth in your area shared the information.

Key Point | Keep hands quiet; keep fingers curved and upright to attain your best speed.

33b TECHNIQUE BUILDER

Directions Key from the software screen. You will practice common letter pairs and then strive to increase your speed.
Goal Increase speed by 2 *gwam* and stay within the error limit.

ws ax sy 4 cows newsreel windows axle waxes relax system psychological fussy

ws ax sy 5 Ryan read a newspaper in the taxicab while going to the symphony.

hu fl yp 6 hunting church thus flair leaflet muffle typical gypsum prototype

hu fl yp 7 Type the brochure for the new florist shop and use it as a flier.

yi sl xe 8 yields frying buying slay outlying flying exempting indexes mixed

yi sl xe 9 The executives vigorously agree to beautifying the grounds first.

33c LISTEN AND KEY

Directions Listen to the phrase, and then key it as a single unit. Key the space following a word as part of the word.
Option Key the phrases as they flash on your screen.

10 see us | if you | as she | my bid | and oil | for gas | upon the | did join him

11 he was due | my key act | we do get | if we do | up and over | was cut down

12 if she is | to do the work | then she may go | to the meeting next week

33d SPEED SPRINTS

Directions Key from the software screen. You will have a limited time between attempts before the next timing begins. Keep focused.
Goal Strive to maintain your 15" speed on three 20" timings.

13 The chair addressed the lay panel but they cut the big endowment.

balanced hand 14 Melanena may amble the shamrock island by bicycle and then autos.

15 With dismay the mentor had bow problems with the official ensign.

37d 1' ACCURACY WRITING ↑↑

A

Directions
1. Take a 1' timing; key from the textbook. If you finish before time is up, begin again.
2. Take three additional timings, keying from the software screen.

gwam 1'

Knowing how to sustain and improve your career on the job is   12
important to young professionals. Doing good work is most impor-   25
tant, but there are other equally important things you can do.   38
Find a modest way to let your boss know your successes. Keep in   51
touch with professional organizations and their meetings. Be in   64
contact with your co-workers, don't retreat into yourself, and be   77
friendly with people in other departments. Do all of these things   90
and you will be in good shape when the time comes for a promotion.   104

1' | 1 | 2 | 3 | 4 | 5 | 6 | 7 | 8 | 9 | 10 | 11 | 12 | 13 |

37e SUSTAINED WRITING

A

Directions
1. Key a 2' writing, beginning with paragraph 1. Key from the textbook.
2. Key another 2' writing, beginning with paragraph 2. Key from the textbook.
3. Key a 3' writing on the entire writing. If you finish before time is up, start over with paragraph 1.

gwam 3'

For individuals about to report to their first day on the job,   4
it is natural to feel a little nervous. But a survey of the na-   8
tion's largest companies reveals a useful insight that should help   13
to quiet those jitters. A sizeable number of executives were asked   17
how many weeks it takes to determine if their firm has made a suc-   22
cessful hire. The average response was twelve weeks; so new hires   26
should not be overly concerned in the first few weeks. Simply con-   31
centrate on learning your job description and how your supervisor   35
wants it performed during those first few weeks.   38

There are several steps a person can take to help the transi-   42
tion go smoothly into a new job. First of all, try to determine   47
what is expected of you; then make every effort to meet those ex-   51
pectations. Get to know your fellow workers, making every attempt   55
to adjust to new personalities that surround you. Seek regular   60
feedback from those charged with judging your work. Learn how the   64
power structure works. You may think it is your immediate supervi-   68
sor; often it is not. See who your supervisor looks to for infor-   73
mation; that may be where the real power is located. If so, re-   77
spect it and don't try to compete.   79

3' | 1 | 2 | 3 | 4 |

Directions

1. Take a 1' timing; key from the textbook. If you finish before time is up, begin again.
2. Repeat the timing 3 more times, trying to increase your rate. Key from the screen.

A

	gwam	1'

When we look at our modern homes it looks as though everything   13
was produced somewhere else and then positioned in the home to look   26
as though handcrafted in place. The availability of seeing excel-   39
lent craftsmanship done on site can still be found, but you have to   53
look carefully for it. I found it in the construction of a salon   66
accidentally. There were no blueprints to examine, just an Italian   80
immigrant who remembered where he was born and worked his design   93
from memory. I'm sure plans were drawn to be scrutinized for mod-   106
ern code requirements, but the techniques he used were never drawn.   119
This is not to discount the development of our modern construction;   133
it's simply to invite you to look for the beauty of true craftsman-   146
ship wherever you can.   151

1' | 1 | 2 | 3 | 4 | 5 | 6 | 7 | 8 | 9 | 10 | 11 | 12 | 13 |

Directions

1. Key a 2' writing, beginning with paragraph 1. Key from the textbook.
2. Key another 2' writing, beginning with paragraph 2. Key from the textbook.
3. Key a 3' writing on the entire writing. Try to maintain your average 2' rate.

A

	gwam	3'

You will be wise to establish exemplary work habits from the   4
very beginning of your first job, including using your time prop-   8
erly. Your record will follow you when you may need a good refer-   13
ence. You should arrive at work on time every day, and you should   17
not leave until the designated end of your work day. Don't always   22
be watching the clock. Follow company policy regarding breaks;   26
talk to your supervisor if the break policy is unclear. Punctual-   30
ity indicates that you value your job and helps give you time to do   35
your very best work.   36

To be a prized worker, you should also learn the importance of   40
organizing your work. Make notes to yourself explaining what you   45
are to accomplish each day; don't have to always be told when and   49
how to perform your work. Obviously, if you don't know how to com-   54
plete a task, ask someone who knows. Set priorities daily, and   58
then you can make quick decisions. Of course, your work should be   62
accurate and meet the exact standards required. Again, this is   67
easier if you organize the work. Write down the deadline for every   71
job and divide all of your responsibilities into categories.   75

3' | 1 | 2 | 3 | 4 |

LESSON 37

Accuracy Emphasis

37a Warmup

Directions Key each line twice from the textbook. Strive for accuracy the first time and try to improve your speed or fluency the second time.

alphabet 1 Hazel quit doing weekly exercises just before seeing improvement.
fig/sym 2 Star (*) Orders #14-38, #25-87, and #36-90 for shipment on 12/10.
accuracy 3 Were you aware your first priority is to write etiquette reports?

37b TECHNIQUE BUILDER

Directions Key from the software screen. Additional practice lines will display if you do not meet your accuracy goal. Key accurately.

uo uy rb 4 Andrew seems to buy barbecues continuously; is that a good thing?
uo uy rb 5 quota arduous continuous guy colloquy buy curb herbicides disturb

wl fy nj 6 You should specify bowling as the game she enjoys for recreation.
wl fy nj 7 owl crawled bowl glorify verifying certify unjust injure enjoined

ya lr cs 8 Politics is involved in the jewelry worn publicly by royal women.
ya lr cs 9 yacht payable yard already railroad ballroom specs topics tactics

37c ACCURACY BUILDER

Directions Key from the software screen. You will have three attempts to key each sentence within the accuracy limits.

10 Do attend every meeting for an opportunity to hear his rationale.
11 We believe we can rearrange my schedule and attend to the matter.
12 She underrated the number who oppose and may reappraise her view.

LESSON 34 — Speed Emphasis

34a Warmup

Directions Key each line twice from the textbook. Strive for accuracy the first time and try to improve your speed or fluency the second time.

alphabet 1 Max was quick to quiz them over big profits in both May and July.

fig/sym 2 Host #123-089 (Andrew) already has 45 signed up for his 7/6 tour.

speed 3 I may pay a man to cut down the giant oaks by the ancient chapel.

34b TECHNIQUE BUILDER

Directions Key from the software screen. You will practice common letter pairs and then strive to increase your speed.
Goal Increase speed by 2 *gwam* and stay within the error limit.

dg xi sf 4 edges fudging wedge exit flexing taxi satisfy transfer successful

dg xi sf 5 Daniel satisfactorily approximated the pledges for the new event.

za ox lv 6 zap hazards plaza oxygen boxing paradox delving culver themselves

za ox lv 7 Plant the yellow dwarf azaleas approximately twelve inches apart.

dm by uf 8 admire landmark admit by baby standby stuff insufficient sufferer

dm by uf 9 The administration will change the bylaws to allow manufacturing.

34c LISTEN AND KEY

Directions Listen to the phrase, and then key it as a single unit. Key the space following a word as part of the word.
Option Key the phrases as they flash on your screen.

10 so few go | he was mad | as it is | if you go | bet he was | were they fast

11 if he | if he is | if he is paid | see a need | took a book | he will state

12 may bid | may bid for | may bid for the chance | may bid for the chance

34d SPEED SPRINTS

Directions Key from the software screen. You will have a limited time between attempts before the next timing begins. Keep focused.
Goal Strive to maintain your 15" speed on three 20" timings.

> **Key Point** The fastest and easiest words to type are balanced-hand words. Every other letter in the word is struck by a finger on the opposite hand.

13 May I sit with the girl by the aisle to clap for the bugle corps?

balanced hand 14 A visitor to the lake may laugh when the clamshells ambush ducks.

15 She held the antique rosy box for a memento of their lame ritual.

36d 1' ACCURACY WRITING ↑↑

A

Directions
1. Take a 1' timing; key from the textbook. If you finish before time is up, begin again.
2. Take three additional timings, keying from the software screen.

gwam 1'

Should volunteer work be listed on a job resume? This ques- 12
tion is often asked. Most employers would like to know if a job 25
applicant does volunteer work. Businesses like to be thought of as 38
good corporate citizens; therefore, they usually value a worker who 52
is a good citizen and who is willing to make a major commitment of 65
time to his or her community. Many employers feel that workers who 79
do volunteer jobs gain skills and also demonstrate a willingness to 93
do more than is expected. 98

1' | 1 | 2 | 3 | 4 | 5 | 6 | 7 | 8 | 9 | 10 | 11 | 12 | 13 |

36e SUSTAINED WRITING

A

Directions
1. Key a 2' writing, beginning with paragraph 1. Key from the textbook.
2. Key another 2' writing, beginning with paragraph 2. Key from the textbook.
3. Key a 3' writing on the entire writing. If you finish before time is up, start over with paragraph 1.

gwam 3'

Most researchers agree on these key concepts about sleep: 4
People should try to clear their mind before retiring; sometimes 8
thinking about problems can get your mind going so fast you can't 13
sleep. People should also attempt to fall asleep each night and 17
awaken each day at about the same time throughout the week, espe- 21
cially on weekends. This helps control various processes in the 26
body, giving us more energy during the day. When we are young, we 30
can fall asleep and wake up whenever it is convenient; but as we 34
get older, getting up at the same time helps us to stabilize our 39
body clocks, improving our health. 41

Studies show that certain hours of the day are more productive 45
time periods than others. For many people, the morning is the 49
ideal time to organize, plot, and do some creative thinking. For 54
others, the evening hours are better. Those who enjoy the morning 58
may be most alert just before noon, but as the day wears on they 63
probably have their lowest energy level in the middle of the after- 67
noon. Their alertness may return toward evening. Those who find 71
the morning difficult may also have a middle of the afternoon syn- 76
drome. However, their increase in alertness continues to acceler- 80
ate into the late evening. 82

3' | 1 | 2 | 3 | 4 |

34e 1' SPEED WRITING ↑ ↑

Directions

1. Take a 1' timing; key from the textbook. If you finish before time is up, begin again.
2. Repeat the timing 3 more times, trying to increase your rate. Key from the screen.

A

gwam 1'

When purchasing a new automobile, all of your senses will be put into action. You view each automobile as a standard for present day modern art and color. The new car aroma is immediately available as you open each new automobile's door. The feeling of new leather begs your hand to touch it again. You hear the engine running, so quiet and smooth. Taste, in this situation, is an insignificant embellishment, not through your taste buds, but in the kind shown by the style and model of the automobile you selected.

12
25
38
51
65
78
91
104

1' | 1 | 2 | 3 | 4 | 5 | 6 | 7 | 8 | 9 | 10 | 11 | 12 | 13 |

34f SUSTAINED WRITING

Directions

1. Key a 2' writing, beginning with paragraph 1. Key from the textbook.
2. Key another 2' writing, beginning with paragraph 2. Key from the textbook.
3. Key a 3' writing on the entire writing. Try to maintain your average 2' rate.

A

gwam 3'

Proofreading is a skill that will continue to be very important when you key any kind of document. You may find that using a spellchecker feature in your word processing software is helpful; however, never just depend on your software to find your mistakes. For example, a word can be spelled correctly but not be appropriate for the sentence. A word such as "the" used where "they" should be used may not be indicated as an error by a spellchecker. Acquire the ability to read your copy from the screen rather than always printing a hard copy to check for errors. For documents to have impact, they must be prepared precisely.

4
8
13
17
22
26
31
35
40
42

If you take pride in all that you key, whether it be the original draft or the final copy, always attempt to find every error. Try to discern anything in the document on your screen that just doesn't agree with the desired end product. Always read for sense, making sure that your final document is exact. Do realize that all of your completed documents reflect upon you. The accuracy of statements made in a document may be challenged in the future, so be sure everything is correct. More importantly, all documents make a statement about the quality of the company.

46
50
55
59
64
68
72
76
80

3' | 1 | 2 | 3 | 4 |

LESSON 36

Accuracy Emphasis

36a Warmup

Directions Key each line twice from the textbook. Strive for accuracy the first time and try to improve your speed or fluency the second time.

alphabet 1 Just next week Hoby's quaint cafes may end regular pizza service.
fig/sym 2 On 3/1/08, $275.40 will be drafted monthly from Account #360-291.
accuracy 3 A logical decision would be to reject a provision in the project.

36b TECHNIQUE BUILDER

Directions Key from the software screen. Additional practice lines will display if you do not meet your accuracy goal. Key accurately.

ng hl tc 4 Pitching in baseball requires athletic ability as well as energy.
ng hl tc 5 range alongside raking chloride highland monthly itch notch match

bj iu ix 6 The moratorium objective was to delay a verdict for sixteen days.
bj iu ix 7 abjure subjoin subjective medium radius sodium fix mixing sixfold

lk lm oj 8 I talked to the patrolmen about projections for this coming week.
lk lm oj 9 alkali walks bulky alms salmon film sojourn turbojets projections

36c ACCURACY BUILDER

Directions Key from the software screen. You will have three attempts to key each sentence within the accuracy limits.

10 They believed the two handguns were used in the fight last night.
11 The news did highlight shortages caused by the idle dock workers.
12 I worked from daybreak until dark sealing the decking on my dock.

Press On

The magic of timings lies in what their results cause you to do. Although not true measures of real skill, results on short 15" and 20" timings suggest your potential and let you know how you are doing. One-minute timings build skill and also help you find ways to reduce wasted motions, work with fewer pauses between keystrokes and between words, and push for new goals. Two- and three-minute timings help you to sustain your skill over a longer period of time.

"The dictionary is the only place where success comes before work."

Mark Twain

LESSON 35

Speed Emphasis

35a Warmup

Directions Key each line twice from the textbook. Strive for accuracy the first time and try to improve your speed or fluency the second time.

alphabet 1 Jackie performed quite well on quizzes over the biology textbook.
fig/sym 2 "Orders #603, #751, #832, and #974 totaled $100.84," he told her.
speed 3 Ryan doubts hymns at my music recital will be much of a surprise.

35b TECHNIQUE BUILDER

Directions Key from the software screen. You will practice common letter pairs and then strive to increase your speed.
Goal Increase speed by 2 *gwam* and stay within the error limit.

xa oe bt 4 exams relaxation taxable noel whatsoever oboe debts subtle doubts
xa oe bt 5 Obtain an example of the exact sizes of blue shoes worn by Julie.

nm hs sw 6 inmate nonmember unmatched paths moths widths swan answer sweater
nm hs sw 7 Government workers take oaths to be answerable for their actions.

eh kl rf 8 behalf reheat behind weekly tickler ankle curfew parfait performs
eh kl rf 9 Jim wholeheartedly was tackling the job of using colorful people.

35c LISTEN AND KEY

Directions Listen to the phrase, and then key it as a single unit. Key the space following a word as part of the word.
Option Key the phrases as they flash on your screen.

Key Point

Dictation is an external way of pacing your keying speed. The objective is to key phrases not letter by letter or word by word. Think phrases and watch your speed grow.

10 of oak | of wit | do fix | go cut | by bus | many own | so big | to end | or bids
11 when they make | when they make them | all agree | we all agree on this
12 you may need to use | a little more effort | to boost your base speed

35d SPEED SPRINTS

Directions Key from the software screen. You will have a limited time between attempts before the next timing begins. Keep focused.
Goal Strive to maintain your 15" speed on three 20" timings.

13 The hayfork is handy for the cornfield and to feed the giant cow.
balanced hand 14 The duty of the chairman is to quantify the profit for the panel.
15 Right now their wish is to work with the firms to make them rich.

35e 1' SPEED WRITING ↑ ↑

Directions
1. Take a 1' timing; key from the textbook. If you finish before time is up, begin again.
2. Repeat the timing 3 more times, trying to increase your rate. Key from the screen.

gwam 1'

Special holidays are so important because they remind us to	12
say the kind things we should be saying frequently to the people we	26
care about. Time for hard-working people seems to pass by ex-	38
tremely quickly, and we justify our silence by telling ourselves we	51
know how they feel. While that may be accurate, most people are	64
like rechargeable batteries. They run down over time, and they ne-	78
cessitate recharging occasionally. It only takes a few seconds to	91
say, "Thanks; I appreciate all the things you do for me. It allows	105
me to be more proficient in the things I enjoy doing."	115

1' | 1 | 2 | 3 | 4 | 5 | 6 | 7 | 8 | 9 | 10 | 11 | 12 | 13 |

35f SUSTAINED WRITING

Directions
1. Key a 2' writing, beginning with paragraph 1. Key from the textbook.
2. Key another 2' writing, beginning with paragraph 2. Key from the textbook.
3. Key a 3' writing on the entire writing. Try to maintain your average 2' rate.

gwam 3'

How well do you get along with others? An honest review of	4
your own social skills is quite appropriate as you look forward to	8
being in the business world on a full-time basis. Various person-	13
nel surveys often reveal that many people who lose their jobs do so	17
because they lack the ability to interact well with their fellow	22
workers. Consider how you have handled disagreement in team situa-	26
tions in your past school and work experiences. Also, contemplate	31
how you respond to authority. Are you defensive, or do you follow	35
orders with a good attitude?	37
We can all develop many personal traits that really are essen-	41
tial in our getting along with others (if we do not possess them	45
already). Analyze your own unique character traits to identify	50
both your good and bad points. On a sheet of paper draw a vertical	54
line down the center. On the left side list your good traits; on	59
the right side list any bad traits. On the left side add the good	63
traits you would like to acquire. On the right side jot down how	67
you plan to eliminate any bad traits. Finally, plan what steps you	72
should take in order to improve your relationships with others on	76
the job. These steps should help you in the business world.	80

3' | 1 | 2 | 3 | 4 |